DYSART

A Royal Burgh

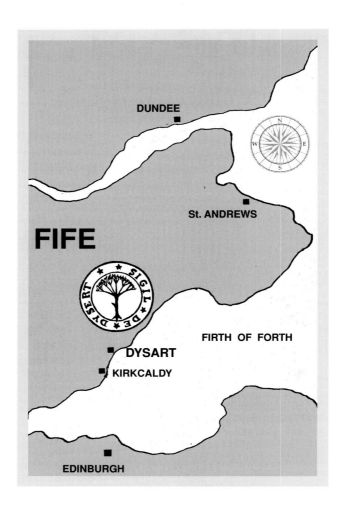

DUNDEE

St. ANDREWS

FIFE

FIRTH OF FORTH

DYSART

KIRKCALDY

EDINBURGH

DYSART

A Royal Burgh

Jim Swan and Carol McNeill

The Dysart Trust

ISBN 0 9530213 00

Research and photographs
Jim Swan, archivist for The Dysart Trust

Text and additional research
Carol McNeill

Published by
The Dysart Trust
01592 641951

Printed by
Cordfall Ltd
0141 332 4640

Contents

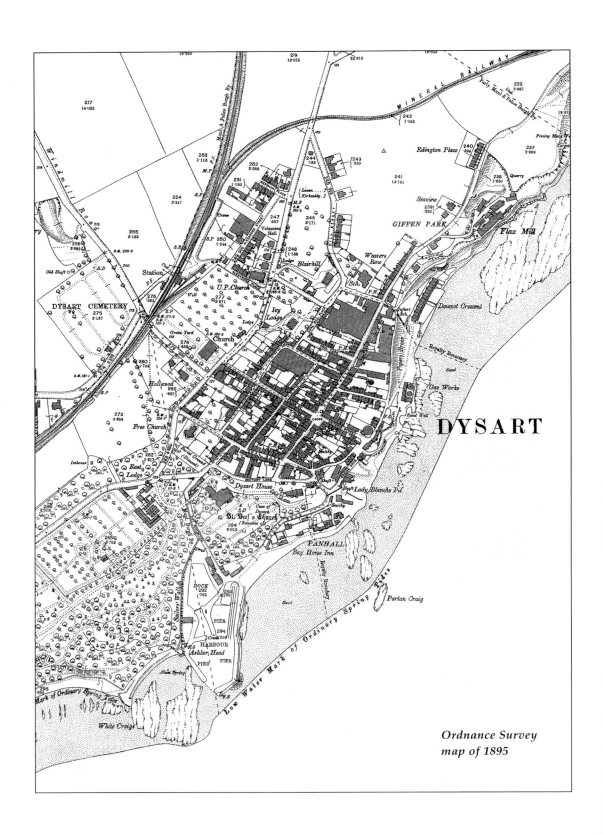

DYSART

Ordnance Survey
map of 1895

Illustrations

Acknowledgements

The authors would like to dedicate this book to the memory of Albert Kidd, a founder member of The Dysart Trust, whose collected material and research forms the basis of the Trust's archives. Special thanks are also due to the 7th Earl of Rosslyn for his permission to inspect his family papers and to quote from his great-grandfather's auto-biography; Nick and Gillian Bromfield; the late Nancy Burgess for her encouragement; Sheila Campbell and staff of the reference section in Kirkcaldy Central Library; Carmelite Monastery; the late Wullie Colville; The *Fife Free Press* archives; Mary and Matthew Forrest; Frank Heggie; Peter Herd; the Meikle family; the Trustees of the National Library of Scotland for permission to reproduce the Charles Rennie Mackintosh photograph and the map of the Salt Pans; National Museums of Scotland; Christopher Normand; Richard Normand, MC WS; Fiona Richardson of Paisley Central Library; David Seager; Grace Swan for her patience and support; Jean Trimmer; Elizabeth Westwater; and the very many other people who helped with information, photographs and recollections

While every effort has been made to trace the copyright of any quoted material, the authors apologise for any inadvertent omissions which they would be happy to rectify.

Jim Swan
Carol McNeill

Chapter I

Early Days

Dysart in Fife is a picturesque, close-knit community on the shores of the Forth, with views of its peaceful harbour, St Serf's tower, and white harled, red pantiled row of houses at Pan Ha' featuring on countless picture postcards and calendars.

Today's peaceful scene is just the latest chapter in the burgh's long and colourful history which stretches back down the centuries like links in a half-buried chain of memories. Although many things have changed over the passage of time, with old customs and industries disappearing and familiar landmarks long demolished, much of Dysart's rich heritage has been remembered and recorded for future generations. And the community spirit of Dysart remains the same, with a fierce independence which has survived the amalgamation in 1930 with neighbouring Kirkcaldy.

The earliest legends centre round St Serf, an early Christian missionary who came to Dysart probably around 500 AD. He is said to have had a fasting place or retreat in a cave on the shore; and most historians take this desertum as being the origin of the name of Dysart.

Another theory says that it was derived from the Gaelic *Dys-ard*, meaning "the height of God". If St Serf's occupancy in Dysart is only a story, it's certainly a colourful one: tradition goes that he had a close encounter in the cave with the devil, whom he expelled from the district after a spiritual battle.

The cave itself is one of several sandstone inlets still in existence in the grounds of what was formerly Dysart House, once the home of the Earls of Rosslyn and now a Carmelite Monastery. In more recent times the cave was used as a naturally cooled wine cellar for Dysart House.

Very little has been uncovered of the earliest history, with little or no archaeological records available. The Romans are said to have set up a camp outside the burgh, but no traces of it have been found.

In common with many communities in Scotland, Dysart's early history was influenced by the church and the landowners. The local landowners were the St Clair family, who created Dysart a burgh of barony, probably in 1483, the date of the oldest existing charter. This was a shrewd move, as it brought the burgh under their direct control and guaranteed them a regular income from the trading concessions and weekly market which they allowed the burgesses to set up. The St Clairs were barons of the burgh from the early thirteenth century, and may – although there are no records remaining – have obtained the grant of Dysart from David I in the twelfth century. Their estates and property included Ravenscraig Castle, one of the first castles specially built to withstand guns, and a mansion house called the Hermitage which was accidentally burned down in 1722 – allegedly by a careless servant who presumably found himself looking for fresh employment shortly afterwards. It was replaced by Dysart House and its policies (now Ravenscraig Park); and the family's influence on and patronage of the burgh lasted until 1896 when the 5th Earl of Rosslyn went bankrupt and lost the family estates through his spectacular life style with huge gambling debts, three wives, and a string of racehorses.

Ravenscraig Castle, 1840.

Burgh Arms.

The exact date of Dysart becoming a Royal burgh is debatable; James VI granted a charter in 1587, but that was more of a confirmation of its status as the original charter had been mislaid over the years. Having Royal burgh status was in many ways a licence to print money, as it granted privileges such as the right to collect custom dues and hold eight-day markets three times a year. The markets were so popular that Dysart became the main market town in mid-Fife, giving an early shopping boom which did the local economy no harm at all.

The Burgh Arms show a single tree with the words *Sigil de Dysert* or Seal of Dysart round it. There are various theories as to what it represents, the most likely being a thorn tree where local regiments gathered before setting off for skirmishes. It could also refer to an old local saying "As old as the three trees of Dysart"; these marked the spot where three St Clair brothers met up on a dark night, mistakenly took each other for a robber, and simultaneously killed one another. It has to be said that the story stretches credibility, but perhaps the nights were darker in those days.

At one time it was a walled town, fortified with a battery of guns which stood on a fort overlooking the harbour as a defence against bombardment by English ships. In 1542 Lord Rothes, one of the neighbouring nobility, asked the Dysart bailies if he could take the guns over for his own use. Not surprisingly, they refused, but he sent a ship from Leith to collect them regardless. It took the combined protests of Lord St Clair and the local magistrates to have the guns eventually returned to the burgh.

Because of its isolated position on the edge of the Forth – long before road and rail links were set up – Dysart was largely bypassed by many of the historical events which affected Scotland as a whole. There were some occasions however when the doings of the outside world did make an impact on the burgh. It may have had its first royal visitor in 1461, as the household books of Mary of Guelders (widow of James II of Scotland) mention the sum of three shillings given to the poor people of Dysart. When she died three years later, the newly built Ravenscraig Castle passed to her son James III, who in a complicated piece of diplomatic horse-trading gave it to the St Clair family in exchange for the Orkneys to bring the islands back under the jurisdiction of the Scottish crown.

There were quite a few royal visits from time to time; James IV came to stay and so did James V and his wife Mary of Guise. In 1545 when Mary, Queen of Scots, was monarch but too young to rule, Dysart was ordered to supply food to a Scottish gathering at Roslin, near Edinburgh. Mary herself is said to have visited Dysart once in 1562 when she was on the way to St Andrews; and tradition has it that she first met her ill-fated husband Darnley at Wemyss Castle, a few miles along the coast.

Many years later, the burgh helped to equip a ship which escorted her son James VI and his Danish bride back to Scotland; and in 1598 the king visited Ravenscraig Castle. After he became king of both England and Scotland in the 1603 Union of the Crowns, James came back to Scotland only once in 1617, when Dysart was told to send two stone-masons to Edinburgh to help repair Holyrood House for his visit. The burgesses were also told to keep cattle ready in case the royal household needed them, and to provide horses to move its luggage across Fife. No records exist to show what local people thought of the royal commands.

*Dysart
Tolbooth, 1853.*

The outside world made its presence felt all too harshly in 1584 when the Plague or Black Death came to Dysart; 400 people died from it from a population of around 750.

The Town Hall, built in 1617 adjacent to the Tolbooth and rebuilt in 1887, was the meeting place of the Provost and Town Council. Among the more colourful-sounding early officials was the doomster, whose duty it was to inflict punishment, often brutally so. The old Minute Books of Dysart Town Council record a man who had his ear nailed to a block of wood for assaulting a customs officer; another was sentenced to the stocks "without meat or drink till sax hours at even"; and a woman was ordered to walk through the town with "horse tails" round her neck.

Women who were suspected of witchcraft were judged by the Presbytery, and around 1640 at least two were burned at the Red Rocks, the natural shoreline boundary of the parishes of Dysart and Wemyss; another was put in prison in the Tolbooth where she took a fatal dose of

poison. By the 1690s, although the charge of witchcraft was still brought, it was more likely to be punished by a fine.

The harbour has always played an important role in the life and development of the burgh since its earliest recorded history, especially in two of Dysart's main industries, saltmaking and coalmining. This was the origin of Dysart being known as the *Saut Burgh*, and its other nickname of *Little Holland* was adopted because of its ongoing trade with the Low Countries, with the burgh's bell-shaped gables and pantiles derived from Dutch architecture. The Dutch influence has always been strong, and one street, Hot Pot Wynd, is thought to have taken its name from the Dutch phrase *het pad* which means the path; the street is a narrow wynd which Dutch (and other) sailors would have taken from the harbour to the town.

Hot Pot Wynd, c. 1906. The two bridges linked Dysart House with Dysart Policies which became Ravenscraig Park in June 1929.

Another equally plausible explanation links it with fires which burned intermittently for years in the coal seam underground.

Both of these industries were operated from the harbour which got its main source of revenue from their manufacture; and when saltmaking finished and coal exports dwindled, the harbour declined and with it, the fortunes of the burgh. By the 1930s, the boom times for industry and virtually full employment for Dysart had long gone, unlikely ever to return.

Many place names which appear in old records have now disappeared. The Town's Garden, for instance, was a large area of ground which was cultivated by local residents probably as allotments for vegetables, with regular rents payable to the burgh. The Bow Butts (below where The Walk now stands) was another source of income for the town, and was used by local militia for archery practice. It was later given to the town piper to graze his sheep on as part of his remuneration, and is still known as Piper's Braes.

Many old buildings disappeared in the Fifties and Sixties as the nationwide policy of "ding it doon" got under way. Whole streets disappeared, with Relief Street, South Street, and Forth Street among the names which are now just memories.

It was partly as a reaction to the drastic demolition process that The Dysart Trust was set up in 1965 with the aim of collecting, preserving and making known the burgh's history – and to watch over its future development. Among the events organised by the Trust are conducted visits to the top of St Serf's Tower and an open-air Church service in its grounds.

Over the years a large number of documents, records, photographs, maps, books and artefacts have been collected for posterity. A selection of these are put on show at exhibitions from time to time, and the Trust is always grateful for donations of material to add to its collection.

Chapter II

The Harbour

Looking at the tranquil harbour scene today with its fleet of small boats, it's difficult to imagine what it was like in the long-gone boom years when tall-masted sailing ships had to jostle for a place to tie up at the pier. Older people with long memories can still recall when the harbour was packed solid with berthed ships; even in the 1920s it was commonplace to see a dozen vessels in the dock and several others lying off the pier waiting for docking space.

These days have disappeared – but so too, happily, have the years when the harbour was closed to shipping and the entrance and basin were badly silted up.

Dysart was recorded as a port as early as 1450 with an export trade in salt and coal, mainly to the Low Countries. There was no harbour as such at the time, with the ships being grounded in the bay at Pan Ha' and loaded when the tide was out.

A natural reef of rocks to the east was later used as the foundation for a jetty, with large rectangular blocks of sandstone keyed into the cut back rock. This allowed loading of ships at most heights of the tide, but it was vulnerable to easterly storms and was often damaged and blocked up.

This jetty, the "east haven of Dysart", eventually fell into such a state of disrepair that in 1615 it was abandoned. The foundation stones are all that are left, and these can still be seen at low water at the largest spring tides three or four times a year.

The present harbour was begun in the early seventeenth century, raising an east pier by again building on existing reefs of rock running in a southerly direction. A map of 1750 shows the east and west piers much as they are today, but the overall structure gradually changed as each generation did repairs or patching over a period of 200 years or so. A nineteenth century plan shows a proposal to put a battlemented turret at one end of the pier, presumably mainly for the decorative effect, but this never got off the drawing board.

The Rev. George Muirhead, a local minister, gave a vivid picture in the Old Statistical Account of 1792 of the huge scale of the harbour's cosmopolitan trade, both in the large number of vessels and men involved and also the variety of cargoes going in and out. "There are 23 square-rigged vessels and two sloops belonging to Dysart, measuring 4,075 tons, value £30,000, and employing 249 men," he wrote.

"There is not trade from this port to employ this shipping. They are mostly in the carrying trade, going out in ballast, or loaded with coals, and bringing home wood and other articles from the Baltick to Leith and other ports.

"A few of them trade from London, Liverpool and other English ports, to the Mediterranean, West Indies and America. Three of them are at present in Government service as armed ships, and one as a tender. As to foreign exports and imports from and to Dysart annually, there were exported 4,584 tons of coal, chiefly to Copenhagen, Gothenburgh and the ports of Holland. Imported from Easterizer, Christiansand, Dantzick, Hamburgh and Bremen, about fourteen cargoes of wood. From Rotterdam, Campvere, Hamburgh and Dantzick, two or three cargoes of other goods (timber, wine, iron, flax, linseed oil, tallow, apples, onions, beer, books, oak bark, linen and yarn).

Dysart Harbour, 1840.

"Goods sent coastways annually are 2,080 tons of iron stone to Carron works, 3,583 tons of coal to Dundee, Perth, Montrose, Aberdeen etc., 1,500 bushels salt to Aberdeen and Inverness, 160 bales of cloth to Leith.

"Imported from Aberdeen tiles, bricks, cheese and butter; from Johnshaven, some cargoes of dried fish. This coasting trade is carried on in small vessels."

An extensive report was done on the harbour in 1819 by Robert Stevenson, a civil engineer and grandfather of author R. L. Stevenson; and after years of debate, work on improvements started in 1829. This work, which took two years to complete, included an inner harbour which, closed by dock gates, allowed ships to load coal at all stages of the tide. This was the first harbour on the east coast of Scotland to have such a facility.

Early account books, giving Dysart Town Council's detailed income and expenditure from 1713 to the end of the nineteenth century, show all the expenditure for the wet dock, including £20 as "the town's subscription for a survey of the Harbour and Intended Dock," and "Dinner for 10 gentlemen when surveying the Harbour and Intended Dock, £2.13/- "

The inner harbour was constructed on the site of a former quarry, and the chisel marks of the quarry workers can still be seen on the steep rock face above it, known as Sailors' Walk or High Brae Head. Colonies of fulmars nest there every year, dislodging loose stones on to the ground below as they scrape out hollows in the rock to lay their eggs.

Sailors' Walk and harbour, c. 1920.

Stone from the quarry was used to build St Serf's tower by French masons who had come over in the fifteenth century to help construct Ravenscraig Castle. The ashlar (square-cut masonry dressed on all four sides) would have been called by the French equivalent, *aisler*, by the masons; and it's thought that this is the origin of the name for the piece of land behind the harbour, always known locally as "the back o' the aisler".

Through the years, storms have played a large part in damaging the fabric of the harbour and its sea walls. Particularly severe damage occurred in 1843 when about 100 feet of the east pier was washed away; and as recently as 1967 the end of the same pier was completely demolished in a strong easterly gale.

The state of the harbour was repeatedly mentioned in the old Minutes, with silting a recurring problem, and many efforts were made to deepen or improve it. As early as 1724, residents were told

Back of the Ashlar, c. 1930.

Back of Ashlar, looking East, Dysart.

to get out their horses and carts to clear the harbour after it was damaged by a particularly fierce storm; and those who had no horses were ordered to pay workmen to help with the repair work.

The early account books also record an ever-present pattern of expense for labour and materials for repairing the pier and clearing the harbour. Payments for cleaning

Loading coal, 1897. A queue of carts wait their turn on the high berth to unload coal down the iron chute into the ship's hold, where it would be trimmed and levelled by stowers employed by the Town Council. Each cart held approximately one ton, and it took an average of 300 tons to fill a ship. There are eleven ships in the harbour on this occasion.

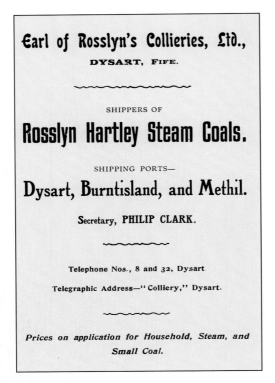

The earliest known photograph of Dysart, c. 1860.

the pier of weeds, wood to repair the pier, driving sand out of the harbour, mason and smith work, are shown almost every month in the local version of painting the Forth Bridge.

A variety of different methods of raising money to pay for harbour repairs and renovations were used, including borrowing £100 from the burgh's "Sailors' Box". Perhaps the most unusual source of revenue was a levy of twopence a pint on ale and beer – something which needed a special act of Parliament passed before it was allowed.

It was a busy, thriving place, the heart of the whole community. Coal from the Lady Blanche pit (situated to the east of Pan Ha') and the Frances pit was exported in large quantities – 800 tons of coal a week were recorded in the 10 years from 1877 – and along with salt from the local salt pans, made up the bulk of the harbour

trade. Ship owners who went to Holland (a major training partner) admired the Dutch style of architecture so much that they adapted and copied it for their own houses.

Ships brought in timber, pantiles, clay for the local potteries, flax, wine and spirits, and left with their holds filled with coal. Cargoes from incoming ships were stored in the Shore House, a warehouse built around 1840 at the harbour at the foot of Hot Pot Wynd. Later on the building, which still stands today, included accommodation which was used by the harbour-master rent free, as part of his wages. It was originally built as a three-storey structure, but over the years the roadway has been built up making the bottom floor a cellar which still has its original cobbled floor, pine beams and floor supports.

Edwin Coatsworth, Harbour-master 1900-1906.

But it was not always all sweetness and light in the administration of the harbour. In the mid-1800s, the Town Council Minutes show a procession of harbour-masters whose careers ended in a variety of sorry circumstances. In 1853, for instance, one was found to be "quite unfit for his duties" after six months in the job; a successor was appointed but in a matter of days "first accepted and then declined the post". The next harbour-master carried out his duties satisfactorily at 10/- a week for the first six months when he even got a rise of 2/-; and all went well for a few years until the Minutes recorded brusquely that "his services were dispensed with."

The Minutes also reported the occasion in 1900 when the harbour-master left the dock sluice gates open after high water, and the schooner *Speculator* was damaged. This incident led to a meeting between the ship's master and the harbour committee when they "endeavoured to come to an amicable settlement of the claim for damages to the ship. The committee offered £25 in full settlement, which was refused." Lawyers' letters flew between the burgh and the ship's owners with some brisk haggling, and eventually £100 was accepted in compensation.

The pilots (who were employed by Trinity House and so did not come under the jurisdiction of the Town Council) were also often mentioned in the Minutes, and not always for the right reasons.

Although by the law of averages there must have been plenty of pilots who carried out their duties in an exemplary fashion, there were quite a few who were downright rogues intent on securing an extra income for themselves. There was a set scale of charges for ships coming in and out of the harbour, but often the pilots asked the masters – especially those who were new to the port – for extra money, and pocketed the difference. The old records have several tales about pilots who were fined for letting ships run aground (one schooner was stranded for a fortnight), or who refused to take ships out of the harbour.

One particularly legendary character was Thomas Cairns, whose pilot's licence was withdrawn in 1883 and then restored while he was put on three months' probation. Four years later, the Minutes said

Three of the pilots who served at Dysart, c. 1900. Left to right – Bob Cairns, Jock Grubb and "Sailor Jock" Smith.

that he had been "repeatedly warned and reported" to Trinity House for his "violent and outrageous conduct". His licence was withdrawn again; but a petition was signed by 300 Dysart people asking for him to be reinstated.

On one notable occasion, Cairns and his co-pilot tried to get more than the standard charges from a Danish skipper as they steered his ship out of the harbour. The skipper objected and produced a revolver which Cairns knocked out of his hand, but the determined skipper went down to his cabin and appeared with a rifle. Cairns and his companion jumped into their own small boat which was tied to the ship, and as the skipper fired at them, they rowed to safety.

The pilots fell foul of Dysart Town Council on several occasions, when it was discovered that ships were literally steering clear of Dysart because of the inflated charges. The secretary of the Earl of Rosslyn's coal company wrote a letter to the *Fife Free Press* of the day complaining about the "extortionate rates of pilotage" at Dysart harbour and spelling them out – much to the concern of the council. With perhaps a dozen ships a week going in or out of the harbour, the pilots made a sizeable income with their extra charges, most of which they spent in the local pubs.

Ships which came in without cargoes were loaded with ballast such as stones and large boulders, which were tipped overboard by carefree crews who were unaware, or unconcerned, that they were blocking the harbour. At first the ballast was removed by horse and cart and dumped on the beach; even today there are many pieces of rock on the foreshore which are not native to Fife. The off-loaded stones became

c. 1900.

such a major problem that a tunnel was later built through the cliff face, with rails laid down for trucks to take the ballast away. The tunnel is still there, a useful short cut from the grassy area at Pathhead sands to the harbour.

The policies of Dysart House (now Ravenscraig Park) ran down to the shore, and in 1896 linoleum magnate Michael Nairn took over the estate and extended an existing wall round the seaward side for more privacy. In addition, his estate workmen were instructed to fill in the handholes and footholds which had been cut in the wall, cutting off free access along the coastal path. Generations of local people had used the path and considered it a legal right-of-way. The new wall particularly affected fishermen who were now unable to dig for bait on Pathhead beach and whose living was threatened. A court action was raised in 1898 to try to establish that the blocked area was a right-of-way, but it was discounted and Michael Nairn was allowed to keep the wall.

Harbour, c. 1920. The buildings on the left were the Swimming Club premises. The pilots' and the stowers' hut are the white buildings on the right.

Local feeling ran very high over the case and the story goes that as the wall was built by day, sections of it were knocked down again each night. Whether this was a token expression of revenge or whether (as was also suggested) it was a canny act by the stone masons themselves to make sure they had a never-ending period of full employment, has never been established.

As is the case with most harbours, tragedy was never far away with many drowning fatalities. Concern grew about the number of local youngsters who were unable to swim, and in 1888 the Dysart

266.

Dysart Harbour.

Swimming Club and Humane Society was established. The Town Council gave the club a piece of land under the shelter of the cliff where a hut was built to provide changing rooms for male swimmers; and more accommodation was added later when the heady excitement of mixed bathing came to Dysart as women were admitted to the swimming club. The club's annual swimming galas were tremendously popular events and were well supported both by competitors and spectators.

During the First War, soldiers were billeted in the huts and the harbour was out of bounds to civilians for the duration of the war. Today the huts are still standing, complete with all home comforts and stoves which generate a good heat from sea coal gathered from the beach, and are used by members of Dysart Sailing Club. Two other small buildings are nearby; the pilots' hut, which was built facing the dock gates about 1870, and the stowers' bothy (built around 1895) for the men who shovelled coal into the boats at the harbour.

Another club which used the harbour was Dysart Boating Club which was formed in 1933; as well as taking part in regattas and races in the Forth, members also organised children's

Dysart Boating Club Membership card.

Digging coal in Dysart Harbour, 1926. Spectators stand on the west pier.

sports days which were held during the Miners' Gala Week in June.

The entire bottom of the harbour was built on a seam of coal, and during the miners' strike of 1926 it was dug out by hand for all-important fuel by the residents. Each family dug their own small pit and at the end of the day staked their claim by leaving their picks and shovels on the spot. Ladles from the outside boiler houses were used to bail them out before digging again, and the women took the coal back for the fire in tin baths.

As the harbour was the town's main source of revenue, it had to be kept in good repair, and this meant constant expenditure. In 1924, the Earl of Rosslyn's Coal Company – the major user of the harbour – put pressure on Dysart Town Council to deepen the harbour so that it could be used by larger ships. The work cost the town £5000, a very large sum in these days. But while the harbour was closed for the work to be carried out, the ships went to Methil and Burntisland docks where they got a quicker turn around – a facility they appreciated so much that they didn't return to Dysart afterwards. To make matters worse the coal company refused to foot the bill, and the whole exercise made the Town Council almost bankrupt.

Deepening the dock, 1924.

Harbour and Foreshore, Dysart.

The sad sequence of events continued when it was found to be uneconomic to try to keep the Lady Blanche pit open; and it was closed in 1929, spelling the end of the main coal trade from the harbour. The Town Council had little option but to close the harbour as a commercial port.

Harbour, c. 1945.

Neighbouring Kirkcaldy had been making moves for some time to incorporate Dysart into its boundaries; and in 1930, with no revenue coming in from the harbour, Dysart lost its separate identity and amalgamated with Kirkcaldy.

After the harbour was closed to commercial shipping in 1929, it was used only by a few fishing boats until the Second War when the Admiralty stored requisitioned small craft there. Redd (colliery waste) from the Frances continually washed westwards to the harbour, despite years of protest and complaints from concerned local people first to the Fife Coal Company and later to the National Coal Board. Because of the huge amount of silt and waste which eventually built up, the harbour lay virtually unused for twenty years, and many people despaired of ever seeing it open to ships again. There was even a proposal in the early 1960s by Kirkcaldy Town Council to fill it in.

The tide turned in 1967 when the harbour was taken over by the newly-formed Dysart Sailing Club which restored it to full use for small boats. It took many years of hard and determined work by club members to turn the derelict harbour into a modern yachting centre. Grants and private donations were obtained to carry out the mammoth task of dredging the badly silted harbour, repairing the east pier, and converting the old harbour-master's house into a clubhouse.

It was a long, painstaking task, but a successful one; and the harbour is now again in full use for small craft as the sailing club continues to flourish. Keeping the harbour clear from the continual flow of redd and other debris is unfortunately a never-ending task, and still has to be carried out regularly by the sailing club at considerable expense.

The harbour has seen many colourful characters over the years, and none more so than the late Will Carr, who was born in 1901 and became harbour-master in 1972, holding the post until he was well over eighty years of age. He was responsible for putting the boats in their moorings, getting them out of the water, and keeping the harbour shipshape; and he also found plenty of time to spin yarns about the old days – even if some of them had to be taken with a pinch of salt.

Entrance to the dock, 1924.

"When I was a lad, I remember seeing the harbour full of sailing ships," he said in an interview when he was eighty-two. "They had to enter port under sail with the tide, and it was a great sight, those three-

to be pulled out of the water so there was a big wheel with cogs. There were chains attached to the wheel and the ship which were thicker than my arm, and it needed about 12 men to walk round this great wheel to move the cogs. They said that by the time the ship was pulled on to the land, the men had walked the same distance as to Burntisland and back again.

Wull Carr, Harbour-master 1972-1984.

The **Jim***, 1937.*

masted big ships with their crew scampering through the rigging.

"I remember when there would be as many as eight tall ships in port, and two or three others anchored in the Forth. Many were foreign ships such as the *Herald*, a Norwegian ship which made the fastest sailing ever from Norway in 48 hours – that's what the crew told us, anyhow.

"I became harbour-master after I retired from the coal company, where I started at 14 as a helper to the miners. We'd go into the pits with the miners; the shafts went out three miles below the sea and we carried a gallon of water for drinking which had to last two of us for the whole shift, eight hours underground.

"The miners earned extra money by working at the harbour. When a ship needed repair, it had

Dysart yawls at the start of the race at West Wemyss Regatta, 1949.

"When the horses pulled the carts through the tunnel, their collars had to be turned sideways to fit through the entrance, but they scraped along the top and left marks which you can still see.

"Next to my hut there was a steep grassy bank leading straight to the water where the women would lay out their washing on the grass to dry. At the back of my hut there was a stone marker over a dog's grave. It had been a mascot off one of the ships, and it got blown into the water with the wind. They got the body later and buried it here, but the marker's gone now, dug up by people who came to shovel sea coal."

One of the first things which the sailing club did was to revive the annual regatta, which has been in existence at least since last century. A contemporary newspaper report in 1876 bemoaned the fact that the

regatta was "a shadow of its former self" and hoped that it would pick up again – so it's gratifying to see that more than a hundred years later, the event is still well supported every Summer. The club's first regatta in 1967 attracted an entry of 120 boats.

In the early days, the boats which took part were yawls and skiffs – fishing boats which were not built for racing but which took part in the event with cut-throat competition. Rivalry was particularly fierce between West Wemyss and Dysart, with supporters following their favourite yawl to whatever regatta it was sailing in.

The yawls (with the name coming from an old Norse word *yol* meaning a small double-ended boat) were around seventeen feet long, and built with larch and oak. Each was fitted with a twenty-six foot mast and a lug sail for racing, and their only ballast was several bags of sand and the weight of the four-man crew. Around twenty-five yawls were built specifically for racing between 1911 and 1953; the earlier boats, built for fishing, were heavier and slower but could still perform well in hard winds.

Two of the best known boats before the Second War were *Barncraig* and *Fleetwing*, both built by master boat builder and miner Willie Burns of West Wemyss. Other well known boats included *Rover*, *Amateur*, *Isabella*, and *Jim*, with the latter (built in Leith in 1901) on display at the time of writing outside the Scottish Fisheries Museum in Anstruther.

Always tests of skill and seamanship, the regattas were originally held just opposite the old Bay Horse Inn at Pan Ha', with great rivalry among local crews. Although some races were won because the boats were lighter and faster, it was mainly the skill of the crews which won the day.

One often-told (and apparently true) story was about a particular Dysart crew who covered themselves with glory in the regatta at West Wemyss and afterwards celebrated well into the night. When they found their way back to the harbour in the darkness ready for the short row home, the oarsmen took their seats and pulled manfully. After two hours, there was still no sign of their home port; and as daylight came in they discovered that no-one had loosened the mooring rope, and they were still fastened to the pier.

In modern times, the sailing club found an ingenious new use for an old disused tunnel which had been originally built through the cliff to make a passage way for trucks of coal from the Lady Blanche pit down to the harbour. (It was a short-lived experiment; this method of transporting coal turned out to be better in theory than in practice, as it crushed the coal in the process.)

When the pit closed, the entrance was bricked up until 1973 when enterprising club members reopened part of it and used it as a boat-building workshop. With electricity wired in from the clubhouse and a fresh-air generator to cut down dampness, it provided a warm, dry workshop capable of housing three boats under construction at one time.

As well as building new boats from scratch, several members of the sailing club have found and restored some of the original racing yawls, rescuing them from dereliction. There are now five yawls back in Dysart out of the original seventeen, along with several other traditional craft, and their appearance in Summer regattas brings the maritime past alive again.

Chapter III

Industries

A well known old rhyme ran "Dysart for coal and saut, Pathhead for meal and maut" and another saying was "ca'in' saut tae Dysart," the local equivalent of carrying coals to Newcastle.

As early as 1450, there were salt pans situated opposite what is now Pan Ha', although there is now no trace of them. It's tempting to look back and think that salt making was an easy industry, and that heating up sea water in pans until it evaporated was a leisurely occupation – but in fact nothing could be further from the truth. The process involved unremitting hard work round the clock, and as late as the 1700s the "sauters" – like the colliers- were bondsmen, just as much the property of the barons Sinclair as the saltpans themselves.

With salt a prime necessity for preserving food, the pans were such a valuable source of money that they were often given as a dowry on the occasions of a daughter's marriage, like the one nicknamed "Lady Janet's pincushion", which supposedly came with a bride from nearby Wemyss Castle.

Dysart had eight salt pans made from heavy iron, each around eighteen feet long by nine feet wide, heated by locally mined small coal; and which according to a contemporary writer needed "a handful of ox or cow's blood or the white of an egg or two" to get rid of impurities. One of the present-day streets in Pan Ha' is named Saut Girnal Wynd after the girnals or granaries where the salt was stored.

The twin industries of salt and coal depended heavily on each other – it took six tons of coal to make a ton of salt – and in the 1790s a third of Dysart's small coal not needed elsewhere was used for saltmaking.

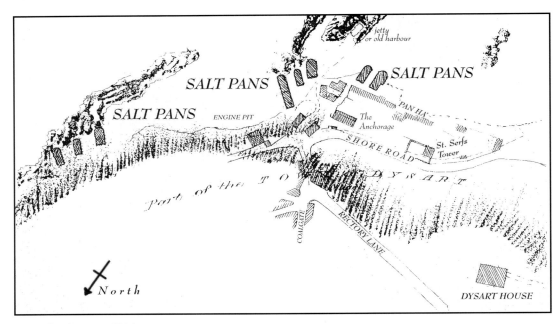

Site of salt pans 1821.

Pan Ha', c. 1920, with Lady Blanche colliery above.

But although the salt industry went into decline when cheaper and better rock salt was imported from Cheshire, the collieries went from strength to strength.

Frances pit head, 1980.

Coal mining is recorded in the burgh as far back as 1424, with Dysart Main Seam running under much of the town and its harbour. Early records show that pollution is not just a modern-day problem, and reports as early as the fifteenth century recorded a succession of fires caused by "evil aire" or carbon monoxide. Smouldering fires and "extraordinary eruptions" continued at intervals over the next two or three hundred years.

It's said that in the primitive days of mining, the monks of St Serf's wove creels in which to gather the coals, and sold them to the colliers for "three bawbees the piece."

The St Clair family owned the mines from the earliest days, and by the 1850s there were three pits in full production – the Randolph, the Lady Blanche (formerly the Engine Pit) and the Francis (its name was changed to the female Frances in more modern times), known locally as the Dubbie. In addition, there were several small "stair pits", forty feet deep vertical shafts with a rough spiral stair inside. These were worked by women and children as well as men who dug out the coal with picks and shovels, with the women bringing it to the surface in baskets. One of these stair pits was located just below St Serf's in the ground behind Bay House, and was filled in for safety reasons in 1929.

Mining was one of the main industries in Dysart for hundreds of years, and as the nineteenth century progressed, miners became increasingly active in trying to improve their conditions and pay. In 1870, when miners were working ten or eleven hours for three shillings

Miners at Lady Blanche colliery, c. 1921. The woman in the centre worked at sorting tables at the pit head removing stone from the coal.

Miners at Frances Colliery, 1942.

a day, Fife and Clackmannan miners formed an association, and almost immediately succeeded in having their hours cut to an eight hour day. A big demand for coal helped them to win a rise in wages to an average of eight shillings, but a glut in the market followed the boom and wages were reduced again.

In 1892, grievances about pay between the coal owners and the miners started to come to a head. Dysart miners discovered that their wages of 4/6d per day were a shilling a week less than miners' pay in other parts of Fife. When the coal owners, citing a reduction in demand, decided to reduce the miners' wages by fifteen per cent, the miners came out on strike. The strike pay of 10/- per man per week and a shilling for each of their children put the men on the breadline; after little more than a month, the strike collapsed.

Matters were weighted heavily against them from the outset as their homes belonged to the colliery owners, and so miners could be evicted if they stayed out on strike. The local paper of the day reported: "The Dysart miners had a long meeting in the Normand Memorial Hall. After a long consultation, it was agreed to resume work on condition that all hands were again taken back. On a deputation visiting Mr Patterson, colliery manager, this was agreed to. A Sheriff Officer from Dunfermline was present in the town with 72 warrants for eviction, but he waited till the meeting was over, and on hearing the decision he did not serve the notices."

Two years later, Dysart miners joined a widespread strike to fight for "a living wage". The local paper reported a "feeling of hostility to those men who have descended the pits for the purpose of working small coal," with one of the workers being followed home and "severely assaulted."

The paper continued: "The demonstration seems to have been pre-arranged, and the excited crowd was accompanied by a band, the instruments used being melodeons, flutes, triangles, and tin cans. The unfortunate victim had a warm time of it, some of the females being foremost in the fray, and his ears were rung several times."

Soup kitchens were set up, with some local firms helping out with donations of money or food. Again the strike was short-lived, lasting for about four months. But strike on a national scale came in 1921, and five years later the miners joined in the General Strike and stayed out for seven months.

In 1923, the Dysart Collieries were taken over by Fife Coal Company which owned them until nationalisation in 1947.

By 1958 the Frances was employing 1,400 men and producing 2,000 tons of coal a day; a section of the pit which stretched three-quarters of a mile under the Forth had one of the highest production rates in Britain. By November 1965, however, there were already rumours that the pit's days were numbered, although this was officially denied at the time.

All that is left of Frances Colliery. The pit head buildings were demolished between 1994 and 1996.

The National Coal Board announced their intention to extend their tipping facilities on to the Dysart foreshore, and Dovecote Cottages (which had been unoccupied for several years) on Piper's Braes were demolished to free more ground on which to dump the redd.

In 1980 the coalfields at the Dubbie – which by then had the distinction of being Scotland's oldest working pit – and nearby Seafield were linked up under the Forth, and although rumours of closure were once more active in 1982, miners were again assured that their jobs were safe.

Miners at the Frances wholeheartedly supported the national miners' strike in March 1984. Underground fires broke out while production was at a standstill, and in February 1985, just before the year-long strike ended, the National Coal Board announced that the Frances was to close with the loss of 500 jobs. Although various plans and strategies were put forward to reverse the decision, it was the end of hundreds of years of coal mining in Dysart.

Another early industry was shipbuilding, with a flourishing shipyard at the harbour reported as early as 1764. Along with the neighbouring sawmill which provided the cut timber, and a nearby blacksmith's shop, the yard produced a very large number of boats over the course of about 150 years.

The shipyard c. 1870 with schooner under construction.

The local newspaper of 1853 reported the launch of the *Ravenscraig*, a 1,000-ton brig built for Kirkcaldy linen manufacturers N & N Lockhart. Adorned with the St Clair coat of arms on the side, the ship took workers to the Australian gold rush three months after it was built.

One of the best known owners of the shipyard was John Watt, who took over the yard in the 1860s to build wooden ships such as fishing boats and tall-masted schooners. Clients came from Dundee, Newhaven, Largo, Aberdeen, Bo'ness, Greenock and other parts of Scotland; and each vessel was launched with celebrations in fine style.

Watt leased the yard from Dysart Town Council for ten years at a time, but in 1879 with four years of the lease to run, he found his business was falling off badly due to a trade depression. Local newspaper reports of the day tell how he asked the Town Council to reduce his rent from £150 a year, something they said they were unable to do. Thanks to the contemporary custom of verbatim reporting of Council Minutes, the debate over the rent reduction was fully documented.

"Every trade is suffering just now," justified Treasurer Terrace; and he was backed up by the Provost who said "This seems scarcely a thing for us to cut and carve upon."

However, a temporary upswing in trade allowed Watt to carry on; and when in 1882 the yard was advertised for lease, there were no bidders. Watt was allowed to take it on again for a year at the greatly reduced rent of £45; but two years later the yard, sawmill, blacksmith's shop and all the equipment and stock were sold by public roup to Foster Brothers.

Although they carried on the business and built a small number of ships, their main work was in ship repairing, and even that dried up after a few years. In 1889 the business was put up for sale and bought for around £150, and by 1912 the dwindling business had closed down for good.

Shipyard c. 1910 with paddle steamer **Conquest** *on the slip for repair.*

The period from the 1860s to the turn of the century was a boom time of virtually full employment in Dysart. As well as the pits and shipyard, there was a thriving textile industry with firms owned by James Normand, Thomas Harrow, and John Terrace manufacturing linen, damask, towels or woollens as well as several spinning mills.

Weaving was already big business in the Dysart area in the eighteenth century, when the work was done on handlooms in the weavers' own homes on large wooden frames not unlike those still used in today's Harris Tweed manufacture.

Because it was a skilled trade, good weavers were hard to come by; and James Normand, who took over a small linen company in Dysart in 1809 with plans for expansion, realised that he would have to do something to attract workers. He built a row of houses with workshops attached, and gave them rent free to the handloom weavers who worked for him. (The cottages which made up Weavers' Row stood at the east end of the High Street, and although most were demolished in the 1930s, a few still remain today.)

A contemporary writer described the early 1800s as "the honey days of the handloom weavers; shuttles might be heard flying in every street, lane and close." But although around 5,000 people were employed in the wider parish of Dysart around this time, the weavers

---

DYSART.

2 *miles* E. *from* KIRKCALDY. North British Ry.
Letters should be addressed "DYSART, FIFE."

FLAX AND TOW SPINNERS AND LINEN MANUFACTURERS.

Harrow Thomas (linen and woollen manufacturer), Monro Power Loom Works ; 90 looms, wool shirtings, skirtings, druggettings, &c.

Normand James & Sons, Ltd. (flax spinners and manufacturers of linen, damask table cloths, towels, checked and striped linen, &c.) ; 2,500 spindles, 460 looms. T.A., "Normand, Dysart."

Smith John (spinner and twister), Dysart Mill ; 6,000 spindles

Terrace J. & A. & Co. (linen manufacturers), Viewforth Power Loom Factory ; 100 looms, damask, huck, dice and honeycomb towels. T.A., "Terrace, Dysart, Scotland."

From Worral's Textile Directory, 1889.

Weavers' Row, c. 1920, with Normand's Mill in the distance.

c. 1899. The large building on the right was Normand's spinning mill and to the left of this were the works of J. & A. Terrace. At the shore on the right is Dovecote Crescent built by James Normand to house his workers, with Dysart gas works on the extreme left.

Looking east from Piper's Braes with Smith's Mill in the middle and the Frances Colliery in the distance, c. 1910.

had to work long, hard hours; and it's doubtful that any of them would have described the times as "honey days". Even by working from four a.m. until eleven p.m., six days a week, they earned very low wages which became even less in the "hungry Forties" when work was scarce and food was expensive.

By the mid-1800s, Normand's business was into its third generation, and the founder's son (who became the first Provost of the burgh) and grandson – both called James – consolidated the company's success. With no competition then from man-made fabrics, the firm did a brisk trade in different types of woven cloth from hard-wearing hessian to luxury damask; and one of their most prolific lines was linen for covered wagons in pioneer America. The first handloom factory was built in the town's High Street in 1845.

It was soon working flat out to meet the demand, although production ran into difficulties as soon as the harvest season came round and many of the weavers took time off to work in the fields. By the 1850s, Normand's first power-loom factory was set up, followed in 1865 by another purpose-built factory in Orchard Lane to supply the growing export market. In 1890 the factory was lit with "the electric light", an innovation which caused quite a stir at the time.

With similar factories owned by J & A Terrace (whose Viewforth factory was built in 1867 near Normand's spinning mill, where the houses on The Walk now stand) and Thomas Harrow (whose Monro Works went up in 1878 beside the railway station), and mills belonging to Thomas Millie (the Old Mill) and Smith (the New Mill), textile manufacturing was big business. Very labour-intensive, the factories gave employment to hundreds of men and women; by the mid-1860s, Normand's factories alone were employing about 750 workers. In those days, child labour was the norm and ten-year-olds were employed as "half-timers" – one day at school, one day at work – graduating to full-time work when they were thirteen.

The days were long (six a.m. to five thirty p.m. with two meal breaks) and the workers were paid once a fortnight. Although the hours of work were long and hard, relations between the mill owners and their workers in the 1890s seem to have been cordial. On the occasion of Miss Terrace's marriage in 1892, for instance, the workers at her father's Viewforth works collected money for an engraved salver as a wedding present for her. At the presentation, Mr Terrace (the Provost at the time) gave each of the workers a free rail ticket for a day trip to St Andrews.

A few years later, Normand & Sons took the forward-looking step of providing meals for their employees who came from a distance, such as Gallatown or Wemyss. "Messrs Normand had a large hall fitted up in connection with the works where the girls could be supplied with breakfast and dinners at cost price," reported the local paper.

*Normand's
weaving shed,
High Street,
c.1910.*

"Tea is now provided at the cost of one half-penny per head, each person providing their own bread. Soup of various kinds is provided for dinner at the cost of one half-penny per pint. Everything is arranged in a mostly cleanly and tasteful manner, and the excellence of the purveying being proved by the fact that there are 150 dinners each day." The newspaper felt the scheme was "worthy of

commendation" as it "diminished the pernicious habit of tea-drinking amongst female operatives."

However, as the new century wore on, the workers began to look for improvements in their pay and conditions. In August 1913, the Dysart Textile Workers' Union was formed with nine main aims which included shortening hours to an eight-hour working day or 48-hour week, abolishing overtime where possible or obtaining extra payment for it, and settling labour disputes amicably if possible. Another objective was to raise wages and "where women do the same work as men, obtain for them the same wages paid to men". This was obviously an important consideration as the first membership list numbered 140 women and 36 men.

Contributions were a penny a week minimum, which would entitle members to a weekly benefit of 5/- if they were dismissed through strikes or lock-outs.

The union swung into action almost immediately when some women workers at Normand's had their wages reduced when they were transferred to other duties; secretary Joseph Westwood (who later became a Labour MP and was Secretary of State for Scotland between 1945 and 1947) was instructed to write to the firm about this, and also to try to have wages paid weekly instead of fortnightly.

Management at Normand's did not seem to take the representations very seriously, as no answer to the letter was sent for several months, even (or especially) when the union also asked for a ten per cent increase in wages. Meetings were arranged to address the workers

James Meikle.

Isobel, Janet and Margaret Meikle.

"at the Orchard lane factory and the old factory and mill." When Normand's eventually replied to the union, turning down the increase, the workers "agreed to give the information to the Press."

The Minutes also recorded lighter moments, with a Social and Ball arranged for members; and an inexpensive way of cutting down advertising costs, when it was agreed "to get someone to chalk the pavements prior to the next meeting."

In 1916 the branch amalgamated with the Kirkcaldy union "for the more effective carrying out of the objects of the meeting." By that time, the writing was on the wall for the linen industry in Dysart. One by one, mills and factories closed down as they lost overseas customers during the Great War, and Normand's went into voluntary liquidation in 1922.

Weaving of a different kind came to the burgh when James Meikle arrived in Dysart from

Lanarkshire in 1919. He set up a carpet factory in Harrow's disused factory in Alexander Street, adjusting the old looms from linen work to carpet, and training the staff in each process required to produce quality material.

The carpets made by the firm were wool reversible, a hard wearing and comfortable product with the added bonus of being able to be turned over when the carpet began to wear. In the early 1930s, Mr Meikle introduced new powered looms for making spool axminsters, and expanded into another site in the High Street, formerly one of the Normand works. Despite the Depression, the volume of trade grew steadily over the years.

Three of his four daughters – Janet, Isobel and Margaret – joined the firm and later became directors, while their sister Agnes became a nurse. Janet Meikle, who started in the factory in 1938, recalled that her father spent the majority of his time on the shop floor rather than behind his desk.

"There was a small office, but he was never in it," she said. "He knew exactly how every facet of the business was going and had all the accounts at his fingertips.

"My father was a very thoughtful employer and took a great interest in all his workers; he was a strong Christian and his workers' welfare meant a great deal to him. It was a place where people were appreciated."

The aftermath of the fire in the High Street factory, March 1941.

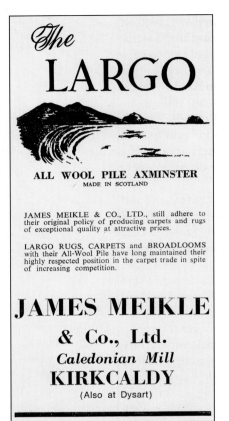

The

LARGO

ALL WOOL PILE AXMINSTER
MADE IN SCOTLAND

JAMES MEIKLE & CO., LTD., still adhere to
their original policy of producing carpets and rugs
of exceptional quality at attractive prices.

LARGO RUGS, CARPETS and BROADLOOMS
with their All-Wool Pile have long maintained their
highly respected position in the carpet trade in spite
of increasing competition.

JAMES MEIKLE

& Co., Ltd.

Caledonian Mill

KIRKCALDY

(Also at Dysart)

*Label for
Meikle's best-
selling quality
carpet.*

James Meikle was Scottish representative of the Carpet Federation for several years, going to London to do battle on behalf of the smaller firms in the carpet industry.

During the war, carpet manufacture was brought to a halt and the older looms were used to produce thick blankets. Many of the work-force went into the services, and some who remained worked in the Alexander Street factory which was temporarily occupied by the McDonald Aircraft Company which made spare parts.

All productions stopped in 1941 when the High Street factory was almost entirely gutted by fire. It happened a week before the Clydebank blitz; if the fire had been a few days later, the flames would have lit up the whole place as a target for German bombers on their way to the Clyde.

The factory was rebuilt as soon as possible, and in 1956 James Meikle acquired the Caledonian Mills (another former linen factory) in Prime Gilt Box Street in Kirkcaldy. Expansion began in earnest, and export contracts were made with around thirty countries including America, Australia, Japan, South and West Africa.

Training in different skills was developed with apprenticeships and night school, with the emphasis on engineering to widen out the existing specialised work. Safety measures were also improved for which the company won awards.

The spinning process was incorporated into the business by taking over a going concern in Tillicoultry in 1964, and after two years Meikle's were both spinning and dyeing their own yarn in Dysart.

"We told our suppliers what we were going to do, because the loss of our business would make a difference to them," said Janet Meikle. "They said that they were quite happy about it and that we were to go to see them if we needed to know anything. In fact, they told us everything they knew; that was the way things were done in those days."

The boom years came to an end in 1976 when for the first time redundancies had to be made in the firm. The business was given to the Scottish Development Agency as a going concern, and the Agency put in a substantial amount of money which helped the business to keep going for another two years. But with a Depression and cancellations in orders, mostly by foreign businesses, it became necessary to call in the Receivers in 1980.

A family firm in the best sense of the phrase, Meikle's is still remembered fondly by generations of employees and local people, and Meikle's carpets are still wearing well in many homes both in this country and abroad.

One of Normand's disused factories was given a new lease of life in the 1930s when Lewis C. Grant moved his engineering factory to the premises in East Quality Street and Orchard Lane.

The firm had its origins in Cupar in 1846 when Robert Douglas started up the business and transferred it to Kirkcaldy a few years later. Mr Douglas took his son-in-law, Lewis Grant, into partnership, and the firm manufactured the American Corliss steam engines, some of which were supplied to the jute mills and rice mills in India. Douglas and Grant then also went on to make machinery for rice milling, but as the firm tried to meet the needs of this increasing market, it overstretched itself and closed down in 1919.

However, it was revived by Lewis C. Grant (grandson of Robert Douglas), who set up on his own to manufacture solely rice milling machines and moved from Dunnikier Foundry to Dysart as business expanded. In its heyday the firm employed around 100 people in various trades.

After Mr Grant's death in 1958 the firm began to diversify into general engineering manufacture, with the rice machinery being gradually phased out until it was discontinued in 1995. Additional premises were obtained at Mitchelston Industrial Estate in 1980, and at the time of writing Lewis C. Grant specialises in precision sheet metal work and engineering products for large electronic companies.

Most of the firm's old premises were demolished for safety reasons in 1996, although part of the building has been retained and is used for the manufacture of commercial vehicle washing machines. The administration and finance departments are still in Dysart, housed in what was originally the manse of the Barony Church.

The family connection is still maintained, with chairman Robin Storie and director David Seager both descendants of Lewis C. Grant.

Another local firm which until recently was family owned and run is William McMillan Ltd in Rectory Lane, which started up in 1921 making savoury puddings and cooked meats.

William McMillan, the firm's founder, began with a small butcher's shop in Mid Quality Street and then moved to the premises in Rectory Lane. These had originally been the stables and coach house of Dysart House, and when it first became a factory, reminders of its previous use were still to be seen with traces of the original horse stalls and the thickness of the stone walls. The entire floor of the building was laid with small bricks (about 3" by 1½"), said to have been imported from Italy by the Earl of Rosslyn. In recent years, however, health and safety regulations meant that the bricks had to be covered over with tiles and then later with concrete.

Mr McMillan and his family lived in the former coach house for many years, and the firm's office was the original bothy where the grooms lived, with the hayloft on the floor above.

The firm's specialities included black puddings, white puddings, haggis, sausages, saveloys and Ayrshire bacon, which they supplied wholesale to butchers, grocers and chip shops all over Fife; and during the war, McMillan's supplied the NAAFI all over Scotland. To begin with, all the processes in the factory were carried out by hand, and in 1950 the first machine, an automatic linker for the puddings, was bought for the factory, with mechanisation in other departments following gradually.

The firm became a limited company in 1942, with William McMillan and his three children Mary, Thomas (known as Harold), and James becoming directors. The family connection ended in 1987 when the firm was taken over as a going concern.

An intriguing mystery surrounds another of Dysart's former industries. When Harrow's Monro Works closed down, the premises were taken over for a short time by a firm called A & G Spalding, a golf club manufacturer. There is tantalisingly little information available about the firm apart from a brief record in the Trades Directory of 1915, and an old photograph of the work-force in the same year. It's tempting to wonder if the present day firm of the same name, an internationally known company which manufactures sports equipment, may have started off in a small way in a second-hand linen factory in Dysart.

The workforce of A. & G. Spalding, Monro Works, Alexander Street, 1915.

Chapter IV

Memories

Life in Dysart in days gone by was very different from the present day – and local people would say that while some things have changed for the better, others have not improved with the passage of time.

Over the past hundred years, Dysart has altered out of all recognition, but memories of the old days are still remembered clearly – with or without the benefit of rose-tinted spectacles. Older people can still remember when the "bairns' bell" was rung at eight p.m. to tell youngsters it was time to go home to bed. We can only guess what the reaction would be from modern bairns if such a curfew were imposed today – but up until the 1930s it was part of the duties of the Town Officer, Geordie Langlands, to ring the bell from the Tolbooth tower which was reached by a small door at pavement level. Not only did the children stop playing and run straight home, but they counted it a privilege to be allowed to help him pull the bell rope.

Geordie also rang the bell at eight a.m. on Sundays to make sure churchgoers were

George Langlands, Town Officer for 50 years.

High Street, c. 1904, looking east.

ready for breakfast and for the eleven o'clock service. An important figure with the town drum, on which he performed an impressive deep-toned drum roll, he stood on the steps of the Tolbooth at election time to announce the results, and to make any public proclamations. He became Town Officer at only seventeen years of age on the death of his father who did the job before him, and was greatly respected for his work over the fifty years he filled the post.

When he retired, the curfew bell was rung by John More, a small man who had to jump up to catch the rope as it came down, and allowed himself to be pulled up with the rope, letting go at the last minute.

Although the bairns' bell is now a long-gone memory and the drum has been put away, the Tolbooth bell still rang for Church on Sundays and on New Year's Day until about ten years ago.

The way of life for Dysart children in the 1880s would be unrecognisable today. First-hand memories of the period were written down by Alexander Logan in the 1930s and published in a booklet, *Recollections of Dysart*, with the proceeds going to Kirkcaldy Hospital.

"School fees in those days were fourpence a week," he wrote, "and every Tuesday we brought our money in coppers or in a silver fourpenny bit and gave it to our teacher. Widows' children had no fees to pay, a concession that was greatly appreciated.

"The law at that time allowed youngsters of 10 years old to go to work as half-timers, and I went to work in the machines department

The Piper's Braes, c. 1900.

c. 1930.

of Normand's flax mill. My wages were 3/3d per fortnight, and as I didn't think I was getting into the millionaire category quickly enough, I left the new mill and started work in the old mill (Smith's) where the wages were 3/9d per fortnight. As time wore on, you worked your way up from the low mill to spinning flat, then to the reeling room when you got five bob a fortnight – we felt we were multi-millionaires by that time!

"We started work at six in the morning and finished at half past five at night, with two three-quarter meal hours between. To augment the household income, bags of hard 'tow' ropes were carried from the mill, and many a night along with our parents and neighbours we sat around in a circle in the home till near bedtime, teasing out the hard ropes, making 'tow'. If my memory serves me right, the rate of pay was 3d per bag."

It was a hard life for Alexander and his contemporaries, with no coats to keep the Winter cold out as they battled through the elements to work with the sound of the old factory bell ringing in their ears – but he insisted that they were happy days. "We considered ourselves great little men and women, wage-earners who were helping our parents," he wrote.

"In the Summer mornings we raced along the streets in our bare feet, and in the dinner hour we rushed down to the sands to the Lady and Gentleman Rocks for a 'dook'. Sometimes we felt very tired at nights after coming home from work, but after a slap-up tea with numerous 'sheafs' of bread and treacle, we were like giants refreshed. If it was not our night for teasing ropes, we were then ready for our games. Our favourite spots were Granny Philp's Close; Dobbie's Close in front of the Store; the old houses where Normand Hall now stands and known at that time as the Rough Corner; and of course the Cross, the Walk, the old Salt Pans, and Piper's Brae."

Memories of childhood before the First War were also recalled by Wullie Colville, who was born in 1906. "I remember the sports day which was held on the Piper's Braes, when we each got three brand new pennies," Wullie said. "The well-to-do bairns had enamel mugs, but us poor ones had tin mugs or tinnies for our milk, and a poke of cookies.

"The Store Gala was another highlight, held in the Three Trees Park (now Ravenscraig) given to the burgh by Sir Michael Nairn. I don't know how some of the Highland dancers were able to dance with the weight of silver medals on their aprons; and for weeks afterwards we were all doing the Sailor's Hornpipe and the Highland Fling.

"Then there was the regatta – what a beautiful sight to see the yawls all lined up at the start, and what a cheer we gave for the winners.

"If a ship was coming in to the harbour, it was a race to get a sixpence for opening the dock gates, and if a boat was to be hauled up the slip by a pole on the capstan, we got 3d.

"One of my earliest recollections was seeing the beach littered with bags of monkey nuts which floated from a ship which sank at the mouth of the Forth – they washed ashore from the Dubbie pit right along the beach to the harbour.

"We used to go up Windmill Road to the Palladium picture house in the Gallatown; it was 2d for the matinee and a comic paper thrown in, and Tommy Leishman who was the manager led us in community singing. The whippet track was nearby and the yowling of dogs was blood-curdling."

Housing conditions in many cases were cramped; overcrowding was a fact of life, and there was nothing unusual in a family with five or six children living in a one bedroomed flat with a kitchen-living room which had a bed recess. But it also meant a close-knit community, with families always ready to lend a hand to neighbours in trouble, and a place where doors were left unlocked for friends to drop in.

Dysart was originally laid out in squares, so the houses and streets formed their own natural communities and boundaries. People took a pride in living in Upper Dysart, Lower Dysart, the Shore, or any of the many other communities, and were identified by the street they lived in. When times were hard during the Depression or the Miners' Strike, people who had work automatically helped those who were struggling; and many a poached rabbit, bag of potatoes, or half a dozen fish were left unobtrusively on doorsteps. Pensioners too, before the days of state help, were also taken care of.

The almost wholesale demolition of old properties in and around   *c. 1948.*

High Street and Town Hall, Dysart.

the High Street in the 1960s put an end to the old squares for good. "Between 1959 and 1970, the whole centre of the place was just ripped out," said one Dysart man. "Whole communities were broken up and entire streets disappeared. Dysart used to have a character of its own; it was a real rabbit warren with houses behind houses, buildings at the back of other buildings. That's all gone now, and it took the heart out of Dysart."

Gone too is the constant buzz of life about the town, when the boom years of almost full employment from the 1860s to 1900 meant a never-ending stream of shift workers coming and going from around five in the morning till late at night.

"Between 50 and 60 years ago," Alexander Logan wrote in 1938, "standing at the Cross at half past five at night when the factories stopped for the day, you would see the High Street teeming with humanity; the workers pouring out on to the streets through the factory and mill gates and passing the Cross in hundreds – old women weavers and young women weavers, men and boys. Swelling the crowd of seething workers would be the weavers from Terrace's factory, but the large majority were Normand's workers.

"Then standing at Orchard lane and foot of East Port, you would see the crowd of workers coming from the Orchard lane factory, all wending their way homewards. At the other end of the town, standing at the Vennel, you would see the cheery Wemyss girls making their way home by the old Weavers' Row, and also the Dovecote Crescent workers going down the Brae – a great sight in those days."

The pits, flax and linen mills, shipbuilding, sawmill and harbour trade all provided work in plenty, much of which grew and prospered because there was little or no competition. Demand for labour was big enough for people to come from West Wemyss (walking along the coastal path) and Pathhead, and the standard of living was on the whole comfortable.

Wullie Colville started work at the Lady Blanche pit at the age of 14 when he was paid 8/2d per shift. "We had seven days off at the Fair week in July without pay, no days off at Christmas and two days off at New Year without pay," he recalled.

"When I started work in 1920, I could have worked at three pits in 24 hours. If you didn't like it, you could have come home at half-time and started in the Lady Victoria at West Wemyss, and if you didn't like it there, there was the night shift at the Randolph.

"When I worked at the Lady Blanche, I used to go down the pit at 5 a.m. and walked underground about two miles to the Frances Pit bottom to collect the three pit ponies and bring them back to the Blanche to start work at 6 a.m. For that, I received the handsome sum of 6d and had to take them back down again at 1.30 p.m. The lady Blanche was named after the Earl of Rosslyn's mother and the Francis after himself.

"I remember once being detailed at work to accompany a ship's captain and crew to the coal face. He was the fattest man I had ever seen, about 20 stone; we helped him into a wooden coal hutch and I had to push it all the way with the three crewmen following. When we arrived back at the pit bottom and helped him out, he rewarded me with the princely sum of a silver threepenny bit which I promptly threw away.

"Another time a captain and crew walked all the way, and when we came to the surface the first mate took me by the hand and said 'Boy, I will climb the highest mast you can find, but I'll never go underground again. That's just for rats and rabbits.'

"Old miners would never wash their backs because they said it weakened them. I remember when the pit-head baths were opened in 1951, that was a real milestone. We were on backshift that night and we were like a lot of playful puppies larking about. We never had so much hot water to wash ourselves before – until then, every drop had to be boiled on the fire or if you were lucky, on the gas grill." (The baths were demolished in 1996 along with other pit-head buildings, several years after the colliery was shut down.)

The link between the pits and harbour was the carting industry. A long procession of horse carts were loaded with coal at the Dubbie Pit and made their way down Normand Road (then called U.P. Kirk Road), past the Black Paling (where the playpark is now), down Back Causeway (Rectory Lane) and Shore Road to the harbour.

The load of coal was weighed at the weigh house and then dumped into the ships' holds. Because the carting of coal from the Dubbie was not contracted to any one firm (as it was in the Lady Blanche), anyone who owned a horse and cart could go to the pit and load up.

"As a boy starting my teens I worked there, driving a horse and cart, and when I first started the rate for the master carters was 11d, later rising to a shilling per ton," wrote Alexander Logan.

"The carters made the roadway cheery with the crack of their whips – and every carter liked a good whip, although more for show than for use, I would say.

"Every day one mishap or more would happen on the way to the harbour, for many an old nag not so sure on its feet would make a stumble and down it would go. But not for long, for every carter behind you was to the rescue in getting the beast on its feet again, for no carter would ever dream of passing a fallen horse.

"Two horses once backed one after the other with their loaded carts into the dock. Luckily in their fall the harness and draught chain broke, making it possible for the horses to be freed from the carts, but even at that it was a job rescuing them. After they were rescued, the two horses were each given a bottle of whisky to drink; and I, being young and therefore to be trusted, was the one who was sent for the whisky. There were some regretful looks and sighs from most of the carters standing round as they saw the precious liquid disappearing down the throats of the shivering horses."

Another mishap was recalled by Wullie Colville. "It was when Andrew Skinner, a railway goods driver, was delivering two big wooden barrels of treacle to Glass's shop in the High Street," he said.

"The first barrel dropped on to the rope cushion all right, but the second one missed it and hit the edge of the kerb, shattering the staves and sending treacle cascading along the gutter. It was like a scene out of *Whisky Galore* only with treacle instead of whisky. Everyone was running with jugs or whatever they could get and spooning it up. We had treacle pieces for months on end and treacle toffee as well."

In the times when days off were few and travel was even rarer, the Miners' Galas were red letter days. Held on the first Monday in June, they included special trains running usually to Edinburgh, with a street party in the evening. The *Fife Free Press* of 1885 reported: "A large number of miners, accompanied by the St Clair Instrumental Band, took part in the demonstration on Monday. The Dysart division reached home about 9.30 safe and sound, all seemingly highly satisfied with the day's outing. After reaching the town, the band played some dance music, and dancing was indulged in by the young folks for an hour or so."

Miners' Gala celebrations were also held locally, with crowds gathering on the Piper's Braes for picnics and children's sports, watching the local yawls taking part in the regatta.

The Gala days continued to be celebrated in fine style until the outbreak of the Second War, with everyone meeting up in the square in Fitzroy Street, where blocks of flats now stand. Many of the houses had been freshly whitewashed and decorated with flags and bunting, and singing and dancing went on until early morning.

With the linen mills working long, hard hours, it was no wonder that the annual Summer day trips – first suggested at Normand's Mill in 1881 – became so popular. It was a day for people to get dressed up in their best clothes and march with banners flying and two brass bands playing. A crowd of hundreds took part, walking from the factory gate along High Street, up the Coalgate and West Port to the station where they would go to Perth or some other town for the day.

Workers at Smith's Mill also had their annual trip, although it was on a smaller scale, and was usually a day's sail on one of the Forth pleasure steamers. Jack Terrace, the linen manufacturer's son who emigrated to Canada, remembered his first voyage which was on a steamer carrying Smith's workers to Alloa. "We sailed under the Forth Bridge, then in the stage of construction," he wrote. "The Italian workmen, who were perched like flies , threw down their caps – or perhaps rivet bags – as we passed."

The golden age of childhood in the early part of the century was recalled by another Dysart man, Bob Cunningham, who was born in

1907. "When I was a lad, Dysart harbour was so packed with shipping that you could walk across it without getting your feet wet some days," he said.

"As boys we scarpered about the streets quite happily in heavy shorts and pullover; nobody ever thought about overcoats in these days. From September to April we wore our boots and went to school in that same outfit, regardless of the weather. Come April, mother would decide it was time to start saving cash, so my boots were taken away and put into storage until next September.

"Oh, the glorious feeling of freedom as you ran the cobbled streets down to the beach and up to Piper's Braes. I think we were all fitba' daft. Barefooted in the sand we would play between the rocks for hours on end, gradually withdrawing inland as the tide came in."

The same golden days of childhood were remembered from Toronto by Jack Terrrace. "Our lives were fully occupied when we were schoolboys, especially during the long days of Summer," he wrote. "The foreshore was our great playground, and we knew every yard of it from Ravenscraig to the Blair burn. We used to make unauthorised entries into the Dysart policies and explore the old Castle, under fear of being discovered by the gamekeeper."

(The grounds of Dysart House with its tempting apple trees still presented an irresistible challenge in more recent times when the house had become a Carmelite Monastery. One Dysart man recalled a day from his childhood in the 1950s, when he and his friends climbed over the wall for apples and were chased by one of the gardeners. "We

Workers from Normand's linen mill parade along High Street on their way to the station, c. 1905.

were terrified we would be caught," he said, "because the story was that we would be locked up in the cellars and made to chop up firewood with a rubber axe. We really believed that, and I've never run so fast in all my life to get away – my clothes were torn to shreds going through nettles and brambles.")

"As boys at school, we kicked a ball of newspaper bound with string; and bools, girds, kites and popguns came and went in sequence," said Jack Terrace.

"The Church soirées were a great delight. Our tickets of admission entitled us to a poke containing cookies, orange and apple, nuts and raisins, and conversation lozenges. We tolerated the musical part of the programme, being mainly concerned with the magic lantern show which was conducted by James Mitchell who was the schoolmaster at Boreland. The moving comic slides were the principal item to us, especially one of a sleeping man into whose open mouth a procession of mice disappeared.

"From the Dubbie harbour to the Red Rocks was where we played most as boys. We spent hours up and down the cascade of hot water from the Dubbie pit, clearing out the ashes to make the streams run faster. We dammed and guided the stream of cold water so that it would be running east one day and west the next.

At the beach in front of the Piper's Braes, c. 1910.

"Through the bushes along to the Red Rocks we made trails and played Indians. At low tide we explored the rocks for partans; we

Dubbie Braes, 1907.

Dubbie Braes, 1929, with the café at the foot of the picture.

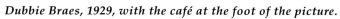

The Cross, c. 1905, with milk carts from one of Dysart's three dairies.

The Harbour Bar on the corner of High Street and Coalgate, c.1906.

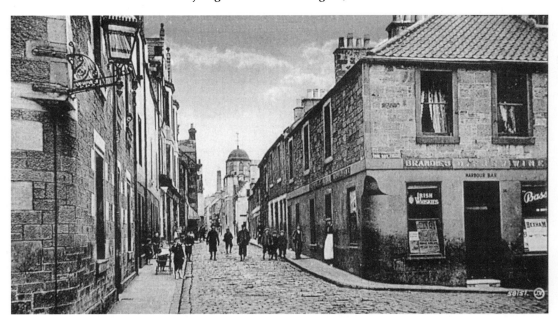

collected buckies and cooked them, and the same fire roasted tatties in the sand below. If it rained, we stood it as long as we could, then dried our jackets in the boiler room at the pit before going home."

There was no shortage of treats available for youngsters who had their Saturday pennies to spend at the shops. Two shops belonging to Geordie Cascarino sold chips and ice-cream, Babbie Barclay's sweetie shop was in Cross Street, with Maggie Blyth's sweet shop next to the bank.

Wullie Colville remembered getting milk straight from the cows from Blair Farm past the Frances Pit. "I used to come up the Back Causeway with jugs for milk at 5 a.m. when Mrs Kidd was milking the cows. It was twopence for full cream milk and a penny for skimmed milk for the porridge. The bigger a jug you had, the more you got – no pints or litres then. There were no fridges and we had to have it fresh each day.

"We really did have long hot Summers then, and food had to be eaten at once. Each house had a spit on two nails which speared the fish to hang up to dry. I've seen the blue flies buzzing round them, but people just fried the fish and seemed none the worse for it.

"There was a wee shop on the High Street near the Normand Hall where Mrs Proctor sold toffee apples and home-made tablet. At weekends she made potted meat and sold it cold for threepence a cup, and if you went with a jug on Saturday, you could have it filled for sixpence with boiled potatoes, and that was our supper."

There were also more pubs to the square mile than in most places, with an estimated 150 pubs at one time in the parish of Dysart (which extended to areas outwith the burgh), surely enough to satisfy the most dedicated drinker. It was no wonder that the Good Templars, who campaigned against strong drink, made such determined attempts to win Dysart bairns round to their way of thinking.

There was friendly rivalry between some of the shops. There were two ships' chandlers, both of which doubled up as grocers; Glass (the only original shop still thriving at the time of writing) and Gibson's, so when a ship was sighted there was fierce competition to see who could get the orders first.

"I used to love standing in Smith the grocer's and sniffing the aroma of the hams hanging from the beams," Wullie Colville said. "Then there was Cheap Johnnie the butcher, who sold only frozen beef which was coppers cheaper; and Maggie A' Things where you could get everything from needles to clothes pegs.

"Another wee shop was Blackadder who sold paper dickies, shirt front, collars and cuffs, and piece hankies – red with white spots to carry miners' pieces for their meal breaks.

"Bob Moffat had a barber's shop in Cross Street and Bill Hopcroft was the soap boy, soaping the men's faces before Bob shaved them. It cost fourpence for a haircut and sixpence for a shave."

*Cross Street,
1912.*

Patriotism and reverence for the monarchy were facts of life in Dysart in the nineteenth century, as in most other parts of the country. Bells were rung and loyal toasts were drunk to mark monarchs' birthdays; the town's accounts of 1806 show an entry for expenses for the King's birthday including coal, allowance to officers, and wine, including "10d for two broken glasses." When George IV visited Edinburgh in 1821, the Town Council had a fair amount of expense putting up a flagpole on the Town Hall and making a flag, as well as "attending the guns at the shore for the purpose of saluting his Majesty as he proceeded up the Firth."

Before the days of hi-tech home entertainment, Dysart folk – like most people of the time – were more than happy to make their own entertainment. Filling their leisure hours was never a problem, except perhaps to decide which entertainment they should choose.

Next to the oil shed on the harbour was a clay bank which was a favourite place for the game of kites (quoits) for the men of the district. The rules were simple enough, with each player throwing metal rings to cover placers or discs which were pinned in the clay. The real excitement came in

Quoiters, c. 1900

Dysart Town Band, 1903, pictured outside the Barony Church.

betting how close the kites landed, and there was tremendous rivalry between groups of miners from Dysart, Cardenden and the Boreland. The games were so popular that crowds of people lined Sailors' Walk above the harbour to look down on the entertainment.

Local people could also enjoy plays presented by the travelling theatre companies at the Fitzroy or Normand Halls or the South School, and in the Summer there were open-air shows at the Engine Brae with acrobats, boxing contests and acting booths. A strong musical tradition gave rise to a succession of bands including the Town Band, the Boreland Band, and the Dysart Flute Band, all of which used to give open-air performances on the Dubbie Braes, the natural amphitheatre below the Frances pit. Dysart Cycling Club, St Serf's Homing Society, Dysart Co-operative Choir (which won many trophies under its conductors John Hughes and Drake Rimmer), and the Amateur Boxing Club were just a few of the wide range of organisations which flourished. Magic lantern shows, evangelical and temperance meetings, concerts and variety shows were all popular events.

The opening day of Dysart Bowling Green, 1914.

Plans to have a bowling green were first discussed in 1880, with a site at Townhead eventually decided upon; and in 1914, Dysart Bowling Club was formed. It was officially opened in June of that year, with Lady Nairn from Dysart House playing the first bowl. The first

president was Provost Anderson who held the position for three years, and the club is still going strong at the time of writing.

One match in the early days inspired the local paper of the day to report: "In one recent game at Dysart, the skip of one rink had a great deal of trouble with one of his players (a grocer to trade) who would persist in playing his bowls short in spite of repeated requests to play them up. At last the skip, thoroughly out of patience, shouted 'For heaven's sake, man, forget that you're a grocer and gie me the richt wecht!'"

The Dysart Parish Horticultural Society, founded around 1885, held its annual show at Ravenscraig Park every August, with not only magnificent displays of prize-winning flowers, vegetables and fruit, but also sports and five-a-side football between teams such as Raith Rovers, East Fife and Cowdenbeath. The tremendous popularity of the event is shown by the treasurer's accounts for the 1920 show, when admission tickets were ordered to cater for 8,000 adults and 2,000 juveniles.

There was also a popular nine-hole golf course in Dysart which opened just before the turn of the last century in an area bounded roughly by Loughborough Road, St Clair Street and Windmill Road.

It was formed in November 1897, with course hazards including a reservoir, disused quarry, roads, and artificial bunkers. Although there

The opening tee shot at Dysart Golf Club, 1898.

was a suggestion that the now legendary Tom Morris of St Andrews might assist in the design, the course was laid out by Robert Nicol of North Berwick. A wooden club-house was built beside the last hole, and the club started off with 100 members (and 28 lady members).

It was opened officially in March 1898 when John Oswald of Dunnikier House (the Hon. President and one-time Captain of the Royal and Ancient in St Andrews) declared the course open. He drove off the first ball, and was presented with a silver-mounted and engraved club to mark the occasion.

During the Second War, part of the course was turned over to growing vegetables as part of the war effort; and in the early 1950s the ground was built on for housing, with streets such as The Fairway now reminders of the golf club.

It was on Queen Victoria's Jubilee that the burgh really let its hair down. In 1887, the year of her Golden Jubilee, the Town Hall, which had just been rebuilt at the cost of £4,000, was officially opened and known as the Victoria Buildings, with an ornamental lamp standard placed at the Cross. The Town Council agreed to send a "congratulatory address" to Her Majesty, the Union Jack flew at the Cross and the town's bell rang for an hour in the middle of the day.

But the council's plans to celebrate the Jubilee with "a cake and wine banquet" ran into trouble. Letters to the local paper attacked the expense which would be involved, and one writer suggested that the money would be better going to the poor. "The Queen has been a

The Dubbie Braes, 1897.

good enough woman, at least so far as we know, but she has been well enough paid for it," he wrote, an unconscious fore-runner of the climate of opinion on the monarchy expressed by others a hundred years later. "I would advise Dysart Town Council to allow this event to pass unnoticed. The over-burdened tax-payer knows too well of the existence of this millionaire lady."

Another letter writer pointed out that it seemed that Dysart was commemorating the event by opening new police cells. "I think that is rather a reflection on the Jubilee year, and on the good name of Queen Victoria, who will be very sorry to hear that more space of this kind is required in Dysart."

In fact, the Golden Jubilee celebration became a three-day event, with a banquet and assembly on Friday, 17th June; a "treat for the poor and infirm" from Mrs James Normand, widow of the linen manufacturer, on the Saturday; and a Jubilee sermon preached on the Sunday.

Provost Terrace was invited to attend the Lord Mayor's Jubilee dinner in London, provoking another local outcry. Not only were the ratepayers to pay for his trip to London, but also for a gold chain of office with the Burgh Arms for the Provost. As it was at a time when the town accounts were in the red, the annoyance felt was perhaps understandable; but the Provost duly attended the dinner and thanksgiving service, and the address of congratulation was given to Her Majesty.

In 1897, the flags were out again for the Queen's Diamond Jubilee which was celebrated on an even grander scale. This time there seems to have been no dissenting voices about expense, and elaborate preparations made it an occasion to remember.

The Dubbie Braes were given an extensive face-lift, with a new path and steps made through the bushes, a concrete bandstand built, and a pond and old wash-houses removed to set the scene for the celebrations. The Tolbooth was hung with flags and banners with the words "Let Dysart Flourish" and "The Queen, God Bless Her."

The Tolbooth, 1897

Cross Street,
1897

The view up Cross Street and East Port was, in the words of the local paper, "like a glimpse of fairyland, banners and flowers being displayed from all the houses, while at intervals to Townhead, large wreaths of evergreens were suspended across the street.

"Nor were the decorations confined to daylight. In the evening, fairy lights were displayed on many of the houses, while in front of Sea View, the residence of Mr John Smith, were fitted up twenty-five red and blue lamps, lighted with electricity by means of a special wire from the mill. On the highest point of the mill, Mr Smith had fitted up a large globe lighted with electricity to the strength of 1,000 candle-power, and which illuminated the whole district."

A local farmer, Mr Steele of Blair Farm, donated a bullock for roasting; and huge crowds gathered at the Cross to see it being driven in a cart to the slaughterhouse a few days before the event. The newspaper report of this makes strange reading in these more politically correct days: "From the time the factories stopped work,

The Cross, 1897.

Farmer Steele and the 'Jubilee martyr'.

the crowd commenced to assemble in the hope of getting a glimpse of the 'Jubilee martyr.' Shortly before seven o'clock the animal, driven in a bullock cart, arrived on the scene and was driven through the principal thoroughfares to the Cross. The crowd was so dense that the cart had to be stopped, and the spectators had ample opportunity to view their prospective dinner. The animal, which is beautifully marked in dark brown and white, had been carefully washed and groomed for the occasion, and was decked in rosettes and ribbons of Jubilee colours."

Jubilee Day itself, 26th June 1897, was of course a public holiday, and after Pathhead Brass Band played the National Anthem and the town bell was rung, the first port of call was the Normand Hall for the now standard wine and cake banquet, speeches, and loyal toasts. Parcels of beef, potatoes, tea and sugar were distributed to 150 people, with a further 100 receiving "from four to five pounds of mutton from the supply provided by the Colonial farmers." School children marched with banners to the Braes where they were presented with Jubilee medals and mugs made in Methven's Pottery in Kirkcaldy.

"Nearly the whole populace had turned out to enjoy themselves in honour of the old Queen," wrote Alexander Logan. "Everyone was catered for, games and racing for the young and old, with the band on the new stand giving out sweet music. There were two large market stalls doing a roaring trade, so that the Braes had all the appearance of a large fair.

"A huge bonfire was set alight at 10 o'clock; it was an unforgettable scene and will always find a place in my memory. At midnight, great crowds led by the band, marched arm in arm to the Cross where a few more reels were danced. Ringing cheers were given for the Queen, 'Auld Lang Syne' was sung, hands were shaken, lastly 'God Save Our Queen' and the end of a perfect day had arrived."

Dysart Town Council, 1897.

1897 Town Council
Standing, left to right:
Councillors – James Herd , Banker and Lawyer, (Town Clerk);
Alfred Patterson, Colliery Manager, Earl of Rosslyn Collieries;
James Anderson, Commercial Traveller, (Provost 1909-1919);
David Mavor, Builder; Robert Blyth, Publican, "The Black Bull",
Relief Street; John Terrace, Manufacturer, (Burgh Treasurer);
George Langlands, (Town Officer).
Seated, left to right:
Bailie Robert Livingstone, Manufacturer, (Provost 1899-1903);
Provost James Allen, Factor, Earl of Rosslyn Estates;
Bailie Thomas Harrow, Manufacturer, (Provost 1903-1909).

Chapter V

Church and Schools

Although St Serf's Cave in the grounds of the Carmelite Monastery is a far cry from the modern idea of a church, congregations had gathered for hundreds of years to use it as a place of worship. Also known as the Rud Chapel, or Chapel of the Holy Rood, it's referred to as far back as 1540 when an old Latin deed recorded a new chaplain being inducted there. The natural hollows of the cave's compartments were made more comfortable, relatively speaking, by seats carved out in the rock.

There was an established church in Dysart as least as early as 1220, when a papal document (the earliest surviving record) refers to a dispute between Dysart Church and Dunfermline Abbey over a chapel in Kirkcaldy (and incidentally demonstrates that friction between churches is no new phenomenon). Other early church records mention a re-dedication service in 1245 by the Bishop David de Bernham of St Andrews, who spent seven years travelling round Fife visiting churches, many of which recently celebrated their 750th anniversary.

Although everyone who visits Dysart is familiar with the landmark of St Serf's tower on the shore, no-one can be sure just when the present building – now in semi-ruins – was constructed. Its eighty feet high defensive tower dominates the foreshore, and has nothing in common with most traditional churches; not many other kirks in Scotland have gun loops incorporated into their design. As well as forming a steeple for the church, the tower served as a lookout and defence in time of war.

The first church building on that site was erected while St Serf's

Cave was still used for regular worship. All traces of that church have now disappeared, and an educated guess can be made that St Serf's was built around the early sixteenth century, with the tower added on to it at some later date.

Early this century, local historians discovered a date-stone apparently from 1310 set into the south wall of the tower. Further research showed that this had been painstakingly done by a nineteenth-century practical joker, confirmed by the Rev. William Muir in his book *The Antiquities of Dysart*.

"A few years ago, some person chiselled very neatly on the old tower, the date 1310. That such buildings were begun or completed in that year I cannot believe," he wrote in 1826. "It was a year of famine and Scotland was then in a humble position, with all our places of strength apart from Stirling Castle in the hands of the English."

The tower was built with five gunloops in the south and west walls, four of them overlooking the Anchorage, one of the few safe landing places on the coast, and also providing defence for the home of the St Clair family.

The first recorded mention of St Serf's church is in a document of 1533, when a meeting of the baillies and the "nybors" was held in the "stepell" to decide how much customs officers could charge for malt.

Old church ruins, 1855.

St Serf's was a fairly large church, built as a parallelogram with a central nave and two side aisles, but without transepts, measuring 142 feet long from west to east and 48 feet wide.

The church survived the Reformation of 1560 with no apparent damage; above the door of the south porch there is still a delicate carving of a vase with three lilies, symbolising the Virgin Mary and dating from pre-Reformation times. The cross loft, where choristers would have sung in Catholic services, is mentioned in Town Council Minutes of 1562, suggesting that the church had moved into Protestant hands two years previously with little or no damage.

Different guilds or trades bought their own galleries or lofts, with the largest one belonging to the shipmasters and seamen who had fifty-nine seats in the church. A wooden panel of an armed merchant ship of 1613, thought to have been fixed in front of the seamen's loft, has been preserved in Kirkcaldy Museum. Other lofts were owned by the maltmen and the tailors, as well as by magistrates and the St Clair family.

Wooden panel from Seamen's Loft, dated 1613.

The manse stood close by the church, built in front of the tower and right behind the Bay Horse Inn, the first in the row of now restored houses at Pan Ha'. According to old reports, it had a courtyard with a carved stone over the entrance with the words "My Hoip is in the Lord" and the date, 1583. The lintel stone can still be seen on the side garden wall of Bay House, as the old inn is now called.

The date stone was probably carved on completion of a programme of extensive repairs by the Town Council, whose magistrates appointed a slater to "turf and theik" the whole church and "mend the hollis."

In 1592 the Town Council bought the town's first clock and put it in St Serf's tower. Its usefulness must have been limited as the clock had no face or hands, but only mechanism and a bell hammer which struck the hours; so apart from hearing the bell being struck, there was nothing to show that the clock existed. It also gave rise to the debatable theory that this was the origin of the old Scots word "knock" for clock.

More repairs were carried out in 1610; but nine years later, there was a riot by the congregation who objected to their minister being deposed for non-conformity by the Bishop of St Andrews, and who took their annoyance out on the fabric of the church.

Like any building, it needed constant repairs. An old invoice from 1715 gives the cost of materials and labour for repairing the church, including 6000 slates which cost £180, "glas work" at £20, 80 bags of lime, and "nails great and small" which costs £60, a total bill of £548 which must have been a considerable sum in those days.

An old Session record from 1747 showed that a Communion season stretched over three days from Saturday to Monday, and elders were appointed to collect at each of the three doors. Twice a year, "fast days" at the start of Communion seasons were held when no work of any kind was permitted and even working in the garden was forbidden. Shops and businesses were closed, and as the enforced holidays were held on Thursday, they were highly unpopular with most bread-winners as they lost a day's pay.

Fast days continued for many years, and Alexander Logan recollected: "The old Fast Day holiday happened on a Thursday, and what a miserable holiday for youngsters as well as older people. All shops closed and business stopped, nothing opened but the kirks for worshippers."

By 1877 a contemporary writer reported that "it was no use attempting to disguise the fact that fast days in Scotland were a farce." The day became more of a holiday, and the custom was discontinued by the 1880s.

Church buildings in one form or another stretched to the east of St Serf's. Stone masons who were rebuilding a wall during the renovation of Pan Ha' in 1969 found an old stone identified as a cresset – a form of crusie or lampstand. About a foot square and around six inches thick, it had nine shallow hollow spaces which would have been filled with tallow and a wick to provide muted light. It was an important discovery and is one of only around twenty such stones uncovered in Scotland, and much more elaborate than most.

The area where it was found may well have been the site of

Drawing of Cresset stone found at Pan Ha'.

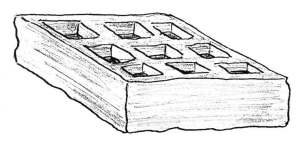

buildings which housed priests or chaplains before the Reformation. Alternatively, it may have been used in the Chapel of St Denis, a smaller chapel which was in existence in the sixteenth century if not earlier, dedicated to the patron saint of France, and possibly also built by French masons. It probably stood just to the east of Pan Ha', near where the Lady Blanche pit was later established. The old smiddy which stood beside the pit is almost certain to have been part of the old chapel.

Supporting this theory is a letter written on 18th February, 1789, by the Rev. George Muirhead. The letter, addressed to someone who had written to his father and himself enquiring about St Denis's Chapel, makes it clear that the building had been ruined for some time.

"We are sorry that it is not in our power to give you the information you wish," he wrote. "All that we have been able to collect from tradition is that there had been a priory of Black Friars at this place.

"Their chapel was named St Denis and had been long in a ruinous state till it was lately repaired and converted to a forge. It is the property of James St Clair of St Clair whose residence is in the neighbourhood. It was situated on the S.W. part of the town, about a gun shot to the east of the parish church, having the sea nearly the same distance to the south and south east.

"What remained most entire of it was a building of 30 feet by 16, two storeys, the under half having a vent in one end. There had been a well in the floor of it, and I have been informed that some people remember remains of vaults at some distance to the north of it."

Some years ago, the ground to the east of Pan Ha' subsided and revealed the remains of carved stones and pillars; but the area has never been properly excavated.

St Denis's Chapel, c. 1780.

Tradition tells of an underground passage linking St Denis's Chapel with St Serf's; and another story says that when workmen were digging a burial vault in the churchyard for the St Clair family, they came across an arch which could have been the entrance to the passage. The burgh's Chief Magistrate refused to allow an opening to be made in the arch "in case the stale air would poison the community," so the existence of an underground link was never proved.

Although some old grave-stones can still be deciphered, time and the salt air have taken their toll. Symbols such as

St Serf's as it was in 1778. The belfry on top of the tower was a suggested improvement, but was never carried out.

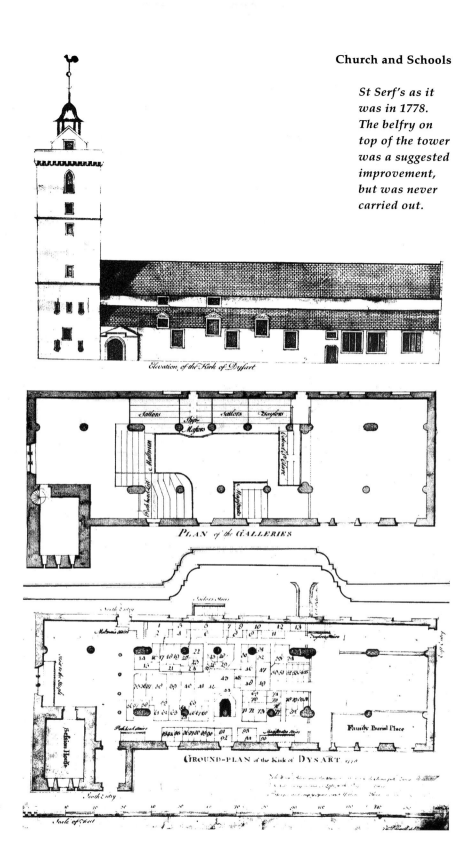

Elevation of the Kirk of Dysart

PLAN of the GALLERIES

GROUND-PLAN of the Kirk of DYSART 1778

anchors, sextants and spades were carved on the stones to record the last resting places of shipmasters, maltmen, and gardeners, while an hourglass, skull and crossbones, or scythe served as reminders of mortality. The gravestones include memorials to James Normand, founder of the linen business, and other members of the Normand family; John Jamieson, former town clerk of Dysart and factor of the Earl of Rosslyn's estate; and James Spence, "dentest to his Majesty," who died in 1783.

But the days of worship in St Serf's were numbered. The Rev. George Muirhead wrote in the *Old Statistical Account*: "The church is dark, the side walls low, with too many pillars, all an incumbrance. It could not seat half the congregation." Plans were drawn up to extend the church but they got no further than on paper, and a new church was built, leaving St Serf's to fall into ruin. In 1804, the north aisle was removed to make way for a direct road from the Engine Pit to the harbour.

The new parish church, Dysart Barony, was built in Normand Road, and although it's popularly said to have been built in 1800, seating 1800, and costing £1,800, it was actually built two years later than that for a total cost of £2,000. Moving the congregation from the church on the shore was quite an event, and for many years afterwards 1802 was referred to locally as "the year of the big flittin'."

Barony Church, c. 1948.

The building currently stands empty after its amalgamation with the present Dysart Kirk in 1972 when it was used temporarily as premises for the YMCA. Its graveyard still remains, with burials taking

place until the late 1890s and a few in the early years of this century. The graves of ships' carpenters, ministers, shoemakers, farmers, tailors, merchants and masons are all recorded, as well as poignant reminders of children – often several in the same family – who died before reaching school age.

As in the rest of the country, the churches in Dysart were not only places of worship but a means of keeping local people on the straight and narrow. Old Minutes reveal a depressing catalogue of familiar human failings stretching down the centuries, with public repentance demanded for those who found imaginative ways of passing the long Winter evenings before the invention of television.

The Kirk Session took a responsibility for the poor of the parish, well before the days of the Welfare State, and many payments in cash or kind were recorded over the years. But by 1841, the Kirk Session found that their funds were too low to pay anything out, and published a handbill appealing to the public to help out.

"The Kirk Session of this Parish," they wrote, "are under the painful necessity of intimating that in consequence of heavy and increasing expenditure, they can no longer continue even the small pittance which the Poor receive without being furnished with more ample means."

They pointed out that Church members or heritors (landowners who also maintained the Church fabric) had already contributed towards the support of needy people – more than twice the amount they were legally obliged to.

"In the course of a few days, every individual will be called upon with a view of ascertaining a voluntary subscription, or whether a legal assessment with all its consequent evils must be introduced."

In 1873, another question vexed the residents, and this was the lack of a hearse for the town. A public meeting chaired by Provost Watt in March of that year was called to consider forming the Dysart Hearse Society.

The Provost considered that "it was a want that had long been felt amongst us, and that some steps would be taken to put the parish in possession of a respectable hearse."

The Minute Books of the Society (which was in existence from 1873 to 1922) make interesting reading, being not so much macabre as strictly practical. Following the custom of the day, the horse-drawn hearse was expected to be topped with black ostrich feathers to add solemnity and dignity to the last earthly journey.

But cost had to be taken into account in this matter as elsewhere; and after a lot of deliberation, the thrifty committee decided to buy a second-hand hearse (which needed some repairs to the top) and to dispense with the feathers for the time being.

Charges were set: "From Dysart to churchyard or cemetery, 3/6d; from Boreland, Gallatown, Sinclairtown and Pathhead to any burying place in Dysart, 4/6d, with non-members in each case 2/6d more."

Despite the financial benefit of joining the society (and tickets were printed "to give to each member on joining the Society to show that he is actually a member"), the non-members who used the service far outnumbered the others. Perhaps then as now people were reluctant to recognise their own mortality by making practical arrangements in advance.

Running the Society was not without difficulty. By 1882, the treasurer reported that the "Links Hearse got most of the Pathhead hires, their charges being 1/6d less," so a reduction in fees had to be considered; complaints were made of the hearse being difficult to turn in narrow streets; and in 1900 there was "some irregularity about the Hearse going out, often unknown to the treasurer." The society was eventually wound up after several years of financial loss.

At the time of writing there are two churches remaining; Dysart Kirk (built as St Serf's United Free Church in 1874 but now Church of Scotland) which amalgamated with Barony in 1972, and Dysart United Free Church in Normand Road, which was built in 1867. In addition, the chapel in the Carmelite Monastery is open to worshippers for services. The Masonic Hall at the corner of West Quality Street and Fitzroy Street was built originally as a church in 1844 for a Free Kirk congregation. Built on a piece of ground bought from the Earl of Rosslyn, it was in use until St Serf's was built and then the building was given by the Earl to the Masonic Order in 1890.

*Dysart Kirk,
West Port.*

Cemetery of St Denis, c. 1900.

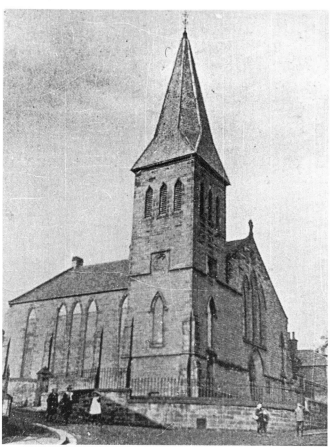

Normand Road Church.

Visitors might be surprised to know that the children's playpark at the entrance to Dysart was once a burial ground. Still known by older residents as the Black Paling because of the six-foot high tarred wooden fence which ran along three sides of the piece of ground, it was given to the town in 1929 by Sir Michael Nairn. Originally known as the cemetery of St Denis which opened in 1750, it was the burial place of burgesses, shipowners and maltsters in the eighteenth and nineteenth centuries. It was cleared of overgrown nettles and grass and the old headstones were either removed or flattened for its conversion to a play area in the early 1930s.

Looking back now, it seems strange that no-one at the time objected to the transition from cemetery to playpark, a change of use which could hardly be more diverse. Although advertisements were placed in the local papers to find out if there were objections from anyone whose relatives were buried there, no-one seems to have felt strongly enough to stop the plan. As the new (and current) cemetery in Windmill Road began to be used in 1868, it seems likely that St Denis's cemetery was still in use until then, becoming a playpark less than 100 years after the last burials. Sadly, no official records of the headstones remain, with only a random half-dozen names known of the people who were laid to rest there. Local hearsay goes that some of the broken headstones were used to build a garden wall in the neighbourhood, a story which is unlikely to be confirmed.

Part of the design of Mackintosh's mural in Dysart Kirk.

Dysart Kirk, built in an unusual clover-leaf shape, hides a secret; behind its cream-painted walls lies a flamboyant stencilled mural designed by world-famous Glasgow artist and architect Charles Rennie Mackintosh.

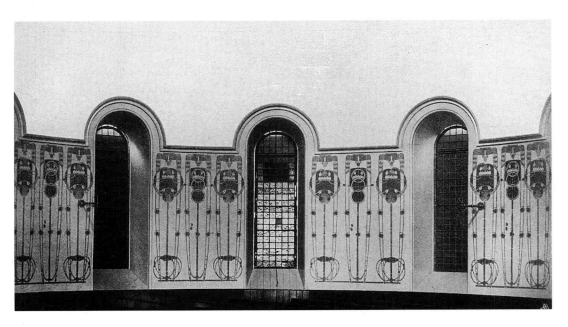

Records show that Mackintosh visited Dysart on 1st October, 1901 (and claimed expenses for his visit from his employers, Honeyman & Keppie); and a fortnight later, the church paid the firm £10 in fees for "decorations." The design showed the dove of peace and the tree of knowledge with three rings depicting good, evil and eternity, with marked similarities to the pulpit which Mackintosh designed for Queen's Cross Church in Glasgow.

Photographs of the design were published in a German design magazine of 1902, and can be seen in the National Library of Scotland; and it is included in all the major references of Mackintosh's work.

Some time later, however, the mural was painted over – perhaps Mackintosh's *art nouveau* style was too rich for the douce tastes of the congregation – and no trace of it is now visible. Perhaps some time in the future, modern technology could be used to uncover or restore at least a portion of this decoration which would now be virtually priceless and of tremendous interest to lovers of Mackintosh the world over.

Just beside Dysart Kirk is the War Memorial, which was officially unveiled after the First War by the Earl of Rosslyn; and a crow-stepped doocot shaped like a lectern which probably kept Dysart House well supplied with pigeons in years gone by.

The Earl of Rosslyn (second from left) in uniform at the unveiling of the War Memorial on November 20th, 1920, with Provost MacLeod in centre.

The church was originally responsible for education in the burgh, and in 1636, Kirkcaldy Presbytery decided that a "gude schole" was necessary. The town was to pay two-thirds of the school master's stipend, with the heritors paying the other third, and parents of the pupils being responsible for supplying his food. The first school is thought to have been built at the foot of the old manse garden, another of the closely packed buildings behind the Bay Horse Inn; and the first school teacher, John Gow, was also session clerk of St Serf's.

By the early 1800s, local children went to burgh schools, or alternatively to private schools which gradually disappeared as time went on. A school board was established in 1873, when the two main schools were the South School at the east end of the High Street (nicknamed Geddes's after its headmaster); and the North School (known as the Wee School) at the top of School Brae which opened in 1873, with head teacher John Boyd and two teachers in charge of four crowded classrooms. (Not surprisingly, there was great rivalry between the two schools with running battles commonplace with both sets of pupils.) There was also the Female Industrial School which probably offered tuition in practical subjects to help its pupils find employment in domestic service.

The official school age was five years old, but younger children whose mothers went out to work were allowed to attend, sitting among the pupils or playing in the corner. Schooling had to be paid for, with fees around fourpence a week for each pupil, although widows' children received free education; and parents often kept their children off school to avoid payment.

Under the Education Act of 1873, headmasters had to keep detailed school records of attendance, absenteeism, illness among staff and pupils, and any other incidents which affected the school. Since careless records could be penalised by losing part of the grants for the school, they were usually meticulously kept.

Extracts from the school logs give some interesting insights into life at the time, showing problems with discipline and truancy, overcrowding, shortage of books, and childhood illnesses which sadly often led to a high number of young deaths from diphtheria, TB, scarlet fever and whooping cough.

Half-day holidays were given for local occasions such as a launch at the shipyard, or national events like Royal weddings, the Queen's birthday, or coronations.

The hard-pressed teachers had problems with unruly pupils, and even in 1879 parents were at odds with the school's idea of discipline. One entry in the log reads: "Complaint made by the parents of a boy about him getting too severe a punishment. The father's idea was that all punishment for faults at school be inflicted by himself." Another entry said tartly: "A parent maintained I had no right to send any of his children after another of his to see why he was absent. It was

interfering with the liberty of the subject. My answer was that the Education Act did most decidedly interfere with the liberty of Her Majesty's subjects aged from five to 13."

Blairhill School.

There were also entries about schoolboys breaking windows using catapults ("confiscated every one that could be found"); stone-throwing; and an imaginative move by some of the boys who "got up what they termed a strike. They nearly all returned by the afternoon. Everyone was severely punished and I pointed out the groundlessness of the step and its utter folly."

Attendances dropped from time to time; as well as illness, there were snowstorms, factory trips, Miners' Gala days, and visiting circuses to keep pupils off school. When a steamer grounded on the rocks outside the harbour and had to jettison its cargo of coal, many children were kept at home to help their mothers collect the unexpected free fuel.

During the Miners' Strikes in 1920 and 1925, the school was used as a free soup kitchen, providing meals for the children; and petitions for clothes and shoes were handed into the headmaster.

In 1881, the North and South schools amalgamated to become Dysart Burgh School, with the infant classes held in the old North School building. In September 1916, the new Blair Hill School was opened and is now the present Dysart Primary School.

Although times have changed and hi-tech aids have taken the place of slates in the classroom, children in Dysart continue to attend the "school on the hill" as their parents and grandparents did before them.

Children photographed in Relief Street, c. 1930.

Chapter VI

The Earls of Rosslyn

The ringing phrase "The Lordly line of High St Clair" was used by Sir Walter Scott in his epic poem *The Lay of the Last Minstrel*, which includes both Ravenscraig Castle and Rosslyn Chapel in the narrative. Although the St Clairs had been landowners for centuries, the earldom was not a very old one, with the title of Earl of Rosslyn being created in 1801. Family members – particularly the 2nd Earl – gave Dysart Town Council quite a few headaches in their time with various wrangles and legal battles.

Although the St Clair family owned a great deal of land in Dysart, including rich coal seams which provided a great source of revenue down the years, the harbour belonged to the Town Council – a situation which often led to arguments. When the 2nd Earl wanted to annexe half an acre of ground adjacent to Dysart House to extend and improve the estate, he had to do a lot of hard bargaining with the Council. Eventually he got his land, but he had to exchange it for several larger pieces of his ground as well as renounce his rights to the site of the shipyard. The Council Minutes of 1808 record his "letter of profuse thanks" for the transaction.

In 1835, he took out an interdict to try to stop the Town Council using the quarry, but the courts decided against him as he had given up his rights to the stone and rock in the quarry some years before.

But in the same year, the squabbles took a more dramatic turn when the Town Council decided to put up a building at the harbour to process whale oil. This was in the middle of the whaling boom, and as neighbouring Kirkcaldy had seven or eight whaling ships which were doing well, Dysart wanted a part of the lucrative business and built an oil boiling house in 1835. Although the Council reassured Lord Rosslyn that "the method of boiling is the most approved one and no nuisance will be committed," he was horrified at the thought of the smell of whale oil polluting his estate.

He applied for an interim interdict to stop the building going up, and when the town carried on regardless, he took his case to the House of Lords. He won; and the oil shed, although completed, was never used. The building was recently renovated by Kirkcaldy District Council and is currently used by Dysart Sailing Club.

In relatively more recent times, Robert Francis, the 4th Earl of Rosslyn who died in 1890, met with the council to define the boundaries between their mutual properties as the plans were "very old and also very obscure." He later agreed to let the town have a piece of his land as a playground – but only in exchange for the shipyard land which his grandfather had earlier relinquished.

When he succeeded to the title in 1866, he inherited an estate of 3,000 acres in Fife worth over £9,000 in rents and coalmining royalties, and a further 100 acres in Midlothian including Rosslyn Castle and its chapel.

The 4th Earl of Rosslyn, 1886.

He was respected as a fair employer who took a personal interest in the welfare of his tenants and workers. He organised outings for his workers and threw open the grounds of Dysart House for a bazaar and musical fete. Every year he and his wife gave £20 worth of coal to the poor of the parish, and many people's memories of him were "pleasant and happy ones."

Contemporary photographs show him looking every inch an earl with snow-white hair, waxed moustache, and a monocle; and as well as carrying out his estate responsibilities he was High Commissioner of the Church of Scotland, Captain of the Gentlemen-at-Arms to Queen Victoria, and a high ranking Freemason.

He enjoyed writing poetry and wrote "Love Lyric to Queen Victoria" on her Golden Jubilee in

1887; and there was speculation that he would be made Poet Laureate. A devoted family man, he wrote numerous newsy letters to his wife Blanche (whom he had married when she was a widow with two young daughters) when he was away on business.

One letter to his wife, however, was more of a reprimand than anything else; he had opened her dressmaker's account in error and didn't think too much of the total. Her excuse that "I only dress to please you, it gives me the vanity of being the best-dressed woman in London" cut little ice with him.

"Such an extravagant cost can surely be little gratification to you; it is sheer unhappiness to me and truly a bad example to your children. The cost of a parasol would keep a family for six months in all the necessaries of life," he wrote to her.

"How nice it would be," he added sanctimoniously, "for you some day to have a little nest egg and say 'I saved all this instead of spending it on dress.'"

Examples of his quick wit in conversation were legendary, including the occasion at a dinner party when a lady asked him if he slept in his eyeglass. "Come and see," he replied, a risqué enough answer in Victorian days and which had the desired effect of bringing the conversation to an abrupt end.

The 5th Earl, c. 1895.

A member of the Jockey Club, he trained and bred horses. He was met in the paddock one day by his stud-groom who gave him the news that a newly born foal had died after being left in the care of a groom who had had too much to drink. "Drunk?" said the horrified earl. "Yes, my lord, drunk as a lord, my lord," stammered the stud-groom. "Drunk as a bloody groom, you mean," snapped his lordship.

He took what was probably a stroke when he was fifty-five, and lingered on for two years before he died, when he was buried at Rosslyn Chapel.

He was succeeded in 1890 by his son James Francis Harry. It was a momentous year for Harry; in the space of a few months he celebrated his twenty-first birthday, married and brought his young bride Violet home, and succeeded to the title of 5th Earl of Rosslyn when his father died.

The young couple received an enthusiastic welcome from local people when they arrived after their cruising honeymoon on the family yacht. "We had over two miles to drive through crowded streets, with school children lining the approach from the West Lodge through the policies to Dysart House," Harry wrote in his autobiography, *My Gamble with Life*.

"My memory pictures almost a conqueror's victorious return, with flowers showered over us all the way, and the escort of the County Regiment of cavalry surrounding us as we clattered through the streets of Kirkcaldy."

Harry was a friend of the Prince of Wales (who became Edward VII on the death of his mother Queen Victoria), who proposed the health of the bride and groom at their wedding; and he was part of the Prince's high-living, glamorous set which was well known in the Nineties. Like his father before him, Harry owned racehorses – his particular favourite was a bay called Buccaneer which won the Gold Cup at Ascot – but unlike his canny father, he gambled heavily. On one occasion alone he placed a bet for £15,000 on Buccaneer to win the Manchester Cup: it lost.

At first, things went well for the new young earl. He was solicitous in the extreme; when his wife was expecting their first child, he brought her doctor to stay at Dysart House to be on hand for three weeks. Before the next baby a year later, he kept an engine "with steam up" at Waverley Station for several weeks all ready to whisk the same doctor through from Edinburgh to be at the birth.

It has to be said, however, that he chartered a train for lesser events. He and a friend, another racehorse owner, ordered a special train to take them from Dysart to York Races for the day. "We agreed that if either of us won our race, the winner should pay for the train, otherwise we should share," he wrote. "We left Dysart at 8.30 a.m., ran in front of the Flying Scotsman, and reached York at 1 p.m. – practically 60 miles an hour.

"We saw four races and were home again for dinner at 8.30 p.m., quite a record. The cost of the train was five shillings a mile, or a total of £125. I paid, because I won the Great Ebor with Buccaneer and Noel's Vampire was nowhere."

His love of gambling took him to Cannes and Monte Carlo, where he lost £7,000 at the tables during his three months' stay. He went to the casino at Monte Carlo armed with £2,000 and bet so successfully on black that he recouped the whole of his losses. After he had cashed in his winnings, he realised he was being watched by two men, and bought a revolver in case there was trouble. "Escorted to the station, we saw the two villains balked of their prey," he wrote. "I returned to Cannes sitting bolt upright all the way, as murders were not uncommon, and to London we fled the following day."

Some years later, he went back to Monte Carlo as part of a syndicate, trying out their system in Ostend first where they won £5,000 in three weeks. They didn't in fact "break the bank at Monte Carlo" although they tried hard.

"We started with five-franc units and won nearly every day," he wrote. "But instead of adding to our capital I kept returning daily a large proportion of our winnings, in my desire to make good to the syndicate. The strain was very heavy, many mistakes were made in the figures, and one of our players was taken seriously ill.

"The system had not failed, for the syndicate were returned 12/6d in the £ and the remainder went in our pay and expenses.

"I can say now that there is no system in the world that can beat the bank, and this one is the nearest approach to any that can make money nine days out of ten, with patience, health and organisation."

His addiction to gambling cost him more dearly than he could ever have imagined. Six short years after he had inherited the title – along with assets of £50,000, lands, estates, collieries, and a magnificent steam yacht – he lost everything with a spectacular run of gambling debts which forced him to declare himself bankrupt. He had to sell up the whole estate, including Dysart House and its policies, Ravenscraig Castle, St Serf's Tower, the Bay Horse Inn and houses at Pan Ha'. The severing of the St Clair family's connections with Dysart House must have come as a shock to the people the burgh, many of whom were deeply saddened by the turn of events.

The family silver – as well as its gold and silver-gilt plate – was sold at a three-day auction Edinburgh, surely a poignant time for the St Clairs. The local newspaper of the day reported: "Dealers were present from all over the kingdom and the continent. Competition was not very keen, but the prices realised were good. The principal item of Thursday's sale was the magnificent Ascot Cup of 1892, designed and executed by Garrard, London. The cup weighs 100 ounces, and bidding was started at three guineas per ounce. Finally the cup was knocked down at £3.13s per ounce, or £438.

"A good deal of the plate was bought in by the Rosslyn family. The dessert and decorative pieces were very choice, and vases of the Medici and Warwick types attracted considerable attention."

The entire estate was bought in 1896 for what seems to have been a bargain price of £30,000 by linoleum magnate Michael Barker Nairn, whose son Sir Michael Nairn later gave most of it back to Dysart. Dysart House, however, was sold by Sir Michael in May 1930 to Mrs Elsa af Wetterstedt Mitchell (who lived with her husband in St Fillans in a house called "St Serf's"). The sale included three cottages, laundry, stables and garages, as well as all the fixtures and furniture but excluding pictures.

A month after Mrs Mitchell bought Dysart House, she gifted it to the trustees for the Sisters of the Carmelite Community. At first glance,

Dysart House

this seems to discount the local story that the house was given to the Carmelites by Miss Coats, a member of the Paisley thread-making family J & P Coats. It's interesting to note, however, that Mrs Mitchell's signature on the deed of gift was witnessed by Miss Evelyn Coats, who was the grand-daughter of the founder of the Coats thread firm. As the Coats family were staunch upholders and benefactors of the United Free Church, it could be speculated that Evelyn preferred to make a gift to the Catholic Church anonymously under the auspices of her friend. In any event, it was a very generous gesture, and Dysart House then became a closed order of Carmelite nuns. It has not been accessible to the general public since the opening day, when queues of local people took up the invitation to see round the monastery.

Harry's marriage to Violet crumbled. His gift of a £2,000 turquoise and diamond tiara to a lady friend was discovered by his father-in-law; and although Harry tried to make amends to his wife, things went from bad to worse. "The gambler's mark was ever on me," he wrote, "the financial position grew worse and worse, quarrels commenced, an undesirable man came into her life, and an incident led to practical separation till we sold Dysart in 1896."

He resigned his commission in the Fife Light Horse when he became bankrupt; and although he tried to rejoin the regiment when the Boer War started in 1900, he was turned down. Eager to get out to South Africa, he got the chance to act as roving correspondent for *The Daily Mail* and at the same time administer the paper's charitable fund for those wounded in the war.

Open day at the Carmelite Monastery, 1931.

He saw more of the action than he had anticipated, including taking part in the Relief of Ladysmith and being taken prisoner on two occasions; and on his return to Fife to convalesce, he wrote *Twice Captured*, a book about his Boer War experiences. It was mainly a straightforward account of his time in South Africa; but in the last chapter he referred to rumours which had been flying around concerning the conduct of one of the crack regiment during the battle at Sanna's Post.

He wrote: "Nor was it pleasant to hear aspersions cast on the fighting qualities of the 10th Hussars and composite regiment, who are reported to have deserted the guns in their mad flight to such an extent that an officer remarked that he hoped the 10th Hussars would never again be detailed to escort his guns!

"Can it be possible? I trust that information on these points will be forthcoming in order to refute the well-circulated story that the whole affair has been hushed up."

All he had intended to do was to air the story so that it would be scotched. Instead it blew up into a row of tremendous proportion, not helped by the fact that the Prince of Wales was the regiment's colonel-in-chief.

Outraged letters appeared in *The Daily Telegraph* about "the statement which appeared in Lord Rosslyn's book imputing gross misbehaviour on the part of the composite regiment of Household Cavalry and 10th Hussars."

A telegram from Lord Roberts, the British commander-in-chief in South Africa, was also published under the heading "Earl of Rosslyn and the Household Cavalry: Indignant Denial by Lord Roberts."

"I am satisfied," ran the telegram, "that neither the Household Cavalry nor the 10th Hussars did anything to discredit their grand reputation during the reverse which occurred at Sanna's Post.

"I personally inquired into the case from the principal actors in it, and I was able to report to her Majesty's Government that 'the troops behaved in the most gallant manner.' Not a whisper of misconduct on the part of any of the corps engaged on that occasion has ever reached me, and his Royal Highness may, with the utmost truth and confidence, publicly contradict the false statement."

Poor Harry; he made a grovelling apology to the Prince of Wales through the columns of the *Telegraph*.

"I owe the regiments whose honour my publication of a groundless report has called in question the deepest apology and the fullest reparation.

"I offer it to you, sir, as Colonel-in-Chief – I offer it to the colonels of the various regiments – I offer it to every officer, non-commissioned officer, and man; and I sincerely trust that this unqualified apology will be accepted in the spirit in which it is offered."

Unfortunately, it wasn't; and he took the only gentlemanly course of action and pulped the entire edition of his book so that the offending paragraphs would never be seen again. But a handful of the books had already gone into circulation, with Aberdeen University Library still owning one of the few copies available.

Harry's mother had grand ambitions for her daughters, and almost succeeded in marrying off Daisy (the elder child of her first marriage) to Prince Leopold, son of Queen Victoria. Neither of the young parties directly involved, however, was keen on the proposed match, and instead Daisy married the heir to the Earl of Warwick. She kept up her royal connections, however, and a few years later (like several other ladies of the time) became a close friend of the Prince of Wales.

Harry's sister Millicent, a strikingly beautiful woman, married the heir to the Duke of Sutherland. It cause quite a stir at the time; three years earlier, her step-sister Blanche was introduced to him with the hope of matrimony by both sets of parents. Millicent, who was only fourteen, went along with Blanche and their mother to Dunrobin Castle for a fortnight's holiday. She sat beside Cromartie at dinner when her knowledgeable remark about one of the family portraits apparently captivated him. Although not many romances have begun with the phrase "Is that a Romney?", it was enough for Cromartie, who never gave Blanche a second thought from then on. He proposed six months later, and they married in St Paul's Church, Knightsbridge, on her seventeenth birthday when he was thirty-two. It was the wedding of the year, with a sparkling guest list headed by the Prince and Princess of Wales.

Harry, despite his literary and domestic difficulties, always took a keen interest in the Dysart Collieries and by all accounts was a considerate employer. He did not allow his miners to work on a Sunday and although this meant they began work after midnight instead of six p.m., he paid them for the shift that they missed. On one memorable occasion, he took his workers for a sail on his yacht to the newly opened Forth Bridge, with dinner on his return.

He felt he was on good terms with all his miners. "I never passed a miner without his touching his cap or stopping and having a crack with me," he wrote. "My house and business room were open to any man who considered himself aggrieved, though I may have possibly been soft enough to undermine the manager's position, which I tried as much as possible to avoid."

He instituted a sliding scale of wages depending on the demand for coal to help make the collieries run more profitably; in his book, he noted how the colliery profits varied from year to year, with the exporting side going from £3,000 a year to £60,000 in war years.

Looking back, he realised how his gambling had prevented business from expanding. "Had I not taken so much money from the collieries in my first five mad years, I might then have carried out my scheme of enlarging Dysart harbour for the export of coal," he wrote. When he was declared bankrupt, he had to leave the board, a source of great regret to him.

Before his divorce, he had taken part in amateur dramatics and joined up with some of his friends to put on "Lord

LORD ROSSLYN'S THEATRICAL PERFORMANCES.

DYSART.

NORMAND MEMORIAL HALL, TUESDAY, 29th OCTOBER.

KIRKCALDY.

CORN EXCHANGE, FRIDAY, 1st NOVEMBER,

At 8 o'clock each Evening.

ON BEHALF OF

THE KIRKCALDY COTTAGE HOSPITAL; THE VICTORIA NURSES (KIRKCALDY AND DYSART); AND OTHER PHILANTHROPIC INSTITUTIONS.

Under the Immediate Patronage of

H.R.H. The PRINCE OF WALES, K.G.
H.R.H. The DUKE of EDINBURGH, K.G.
PROVOST and MAGISTRATES of KIRKCALDY.
The PROVOST and MAGISTRATES of DYSART.
DUKE and DUCHESS of SUTHERLAND.
BLANCHE COUNTESS of ROSSLYN.
Mr and Lady LILIAN WEMYSS.
Mr and Lady HELEN FERGUSON of RAITH.
John OSWALD, Esq., of DUNNIKIER.
And Many Others.

THE FAMOUS PLAY, IN FOUR ACTS, OF

DIPLOMACY.

IN WHICH THE CHIEF CHARACTERS WILL BE—

COMTESSE ZICKA..................Mrs W. JAMES.
DORA.............................Mrs GLYN.
MARQUISE DE RIO ZARES..........Lady MARJORIBANKS.
LADY HENRY FAIRFAX............Miss LINA OSWALD.
MION..........Miss SHEPHERD of ROSSEND CASTLE.
HENRY BEAUCLERC...............EARL of KILMOREY.
JULIAN BEAUCLERC...............EARL of ROSSLYN.
COUNT ORLOFF..................CAPTAIN JEFCOCK.
ALGY FAIRFAX..................Mr LEO TREVIOR.
ANTOINE......................Mr W. JAMES.
BARON STEIN..................Mr C. P. COLNAGHI.

TICKETS.— Reserved Seats, Numbered, 10/- and 5/- to be had as follows :—For Kirkcaldy, at Messrs Burt's and Fergus, Booksellers ; for Dysart, at Mr Owler's, Bookseller, and Miss Buist (Post Office), and at Mr Allan's, Chemist, Pathhead (for both places). Unreserved Tickets, 3/-, 2/6, 2/-, and 1/-, also to be had as above.

CLARKSON'S, of London, SUPPLY the SCENERY and WIGS.

BOOK EARLY FOR A WONDERFUL PERFORMANCE.

From **Fife Free Press**, *19th October, 1895.*

Rosslyn's Theatrical Performances." These were held in the Normand Hall as well as in the Corn Exchange in Kirkcaldy and the Empire Palace Theatre in Edinburgh, in aid of Kirkcaldy Cottage Hospital and the Victoria Nurses (Kirkcaldy and Dysart).

He put on a four-act play, *Diplomacy*, in which he played one of the leading roles. It received glowing reports in the papers, with his own performance described as "exceedingly good; his acting was sound and unaffected, and contributed greatly to the success of the piece."

To make ends meet after his bankruptcy, he drew on his amateur experience and joined a touring company, carving out a career for himself as an actor. It was a phase in his life which he seems to have enjoyed enormously, although not all his friends approved. "Of course the Prince of Wales has been none too pleased at my taking up an actor's career, and if we ever met was quite cold to me," he noted. (In retrospect this seems rather hypocritical, given the enduring nature of the friendship between the Prince and actress Lily Langtry.)

He toured with *Trelawny of the Wells* in Newcastle, Glasgow, Edinburgh, Liverpool and Manchester; and revisited the Normand Hall with *Diplomacy* for a two-night run in front of many of his former tenants and workers.

It was while he was following his acting career that he met his second wife Anna, an actress and American heiress, and married her within a few days. The marriage was a disaster, an "act of rash folly" as he later said; although a charming companion at first, she was (according to her new husband) given to drugs and drink.

"We gave a small lunch party after the marriage ceremony, and immediately afterwards she fell down in a dead faint," he wrote. "I sent for her doctor, whose only remark when he had seen her was 'I suppose you know you have married a dipsomaniac?'"

The unhappy experience did not, however, put him off women, many of whom were in the words of the music hall song "just wild about Harry." He admitted: "How many people have said to me 'What a fatal fascination you have for women, Harry!' and how often have I replied 'You mean what a fatal fascination women have for me!' – a very different story."

In 1908, a year after his second divorce, he met Vera (nicknamed Tommy), who was to become his third wife. Given his track record and "impoverished condition", he was hesitant about asking her to marry him.

"Everyone thought that any marriage of mine must end hopelessly, and there were good reasons," he wrote. "But in my case I found the only lucky gamble of my life when this divine girl married me." Tommy not only married him but stood by her man despite more gambling, rumours of a Russian lady friend, and another bankruptcy.

By 1914 he was reinstated as a director the collieries, and made several innovations in the pits. These included a system of pouring strengthening concrete into the shafts to get more coal out (a method he had seen working in Germany), and a screening plant for the Randolph Pit to grade the different classes of coal.

At the end of the First War, he held a review in front of the Normand Hall for 320 soldiers (many of them miners), presented them with a medal, and entertained them to a dinner and dance afterwards.

After the miners' strike in 1921, he travelled to the continent to find new markets for his coal. "I set up my office in Paris at the Hotel du Rhin," he wrote, "where, with a telephone and a secretary, I received many of the largest coal importers and ladled out an enormous quantity of cocktails."

In 1923, the Rosslyn Collieries were sold to the Fife Coal Company, and as chairman he received "the biggest cheques I have ever seen" for the sale of his shares and a handsome bonus from the directors.

"So ended the lifelong association between myself and at least three generations of my forebears, with the miners of the Kingdom of Fife, unless perchance in 40 years when the lease falls in, I shall be alive to receive the 'ashes' back!" he wrote. "I have been to Dysart, but hardly dare face the old workers. I feel a deserter, and only the success of the sale, when I note the difficulties of the trade just now, seems to have justified me in parting with the greatest asset ever known."

Even when he was no longer living in Dysart, he still kept in touch. An old resident recalled: "I remember when I was a boy helping my grandmother to sell fish. We were in Fitzroy Street when this tall

The 5th Earl in Dysart, September 1934, to crown the Dysart Queen, Nancy Millar.

gentleman, beautifully dressed, crossed the street and took her by the shoulders and greeted her like an old friend. He asked her how the boys were, my father and uncles Bill, John, Dave and Archie. I didn't know who he was, and when he left, he shook her hand. 'Who was that?' I asked her. 'The Earl of Rosslyn,' she said, and held out her hand showing two golden sovereigns among the fish scales; and I never saw it done."

Harry died in 1939, surely the most colourful member of the St Clair family. His eldest son and heir had died before him, and he was succeeded by his grandson, Anthony.

Peter St Clair-Erskine, the 7th and current earl, is a member of Thames Valley Police and is married with two sons and two daughters; so the Lordly line of High St Clair seems set to continue.

Chapter VII

Landmarks

In common with countless other towns and cities in Scotland, Dysart lost a great deal of its original housing and architecture in the Fifties and Sixties.

The need for post-war housing was coupled with the desire for progress; and the result (according to opinion) was either modern-

Dysart High Street looking west, 1912

High Street and Town Hall, Dysart.

isation and improvement, or demolition on an almost savage scale as old houses were bulldozed down and whole streets disappeared in clouds of rubble

At the time, as letters to the local paper in the 1960s showed, residents were sharply divided on the issue of conservation versus demolition. Phrases like "vermin infested slums" battled with "historic buildings and old-worlde streets"; but with hindsight, which is of course a fine thing, it's fairly safe to assume that most people didn't realise just how much the character of their town would be changed.

Reports by nineteenth century writers who described the High Street as having "a number of antique substantial houses, having dates and inscriptions on the front" make wry reading now, as these have virtually all disappeared.

Allowing old property to deteriorate past the point of no return is not merely a modern failing; a report in the local paper in 1884 commented: "Some of the old houses at the west end of Dysart are going fast to decay, and no wonder when we consider their age. The roof of one of these tenements recently fell in with a crash, and the sooner it is razed to the ground, the better it will be for all parties concerned. The house is nearly three centuries old, having been built in 1597."

Co-op bakery cart at the Store Pend, c. 1910.

Obviously some modernisation over the years was essential ; not long after the amalgamation, Kirkcaldy Town Council Minutes of 1933 reported that there were 77 insanitary houses in Dysart occupied by 312 people, and at the same time several areas were inspected and considered as sites for new building work.

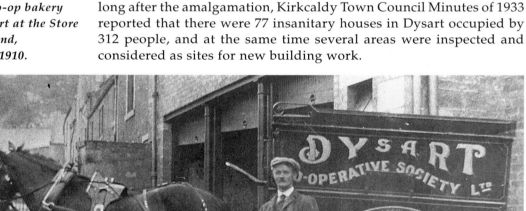

During the Twenties there was no shortage of shops which sold just about everything families would ever need without having to go outwith the burgh. They were all privately owned, with the exception of Dysart Co-op which had a grocery, bakery, hardware and butchery. The butcher's shop had a set of magnificent painted ceramic tiles which showed a succession of local scenes from West Wemyss chapel gardens to Ravenscraig Castle. Although the shop has been demolished, the tiles have been saved for posterity.

Other well patronised shops included Wilkie's bakery; Dick's Co-op whose dividend was said to be threepence in the £ more than Dysart Co-op; Kate Duncan's china shop; Witherspoon, painter and decorator; and Swinley's barber's shop. There was a chemist's shop owned by pharmacist Mariebelle Nekola, whose artist father Karel from Bohemia originated the legendary designs for Wemyss Ware at Robert Heron's pottery in nearby Gallatown. Ladies could choose their outfits from the Duff sisters or Miss Harrow, or buy their hats at Mrs Mavor's, with Mitchell's outfitters supplying men's clothes. Drysdale's smiddy stood in a pend off the High Street opposite Glass's shop, and there were stables there until the early 1930s when the Lady Blanche pit closed, putting an end to the carting industry.

Among other fondly remembered shops were Baxter and Brown's, Annie Laing, hairdressers Jenny and Jean Grubb, Ramsay's sweet shop, Owler's newsagent's, Fairfull the chemist, Robb's ironmongery, Penman's fish and chip shop, McLeod the saddler's, and Smith's bakery.

c. 1920.

The Cat Tavern, with a large tortoiseshell cat painted on the wall, was at the far end of the High Street opposite the Normand Memorial Hall. The Royal Burgh Tavern in Forth Street, run by the Hopcroft family, gave itself airs by displaying the Royal coat of arms above its door and a sign saying "By Royal Warrant from His Majesty King George V." This flight of fancy was rewarded by a large fine from the authorities who ordered the plaque to be removed, and the pub's name was downgraded to the Forth Tavern.

A Civic Survey of Kirkcaldy and Dysart carried out in 1950 described Dysart as having a "very strong community feeling" and warned that care should be taken in redeveloping the area to ensure that the character of the old burgh was not lost.

It has to be assumed that the powers-that-be didn't read that part of the report, as countless houses were demolished and several streets disappeared. Comparisons with other old Fife burghs such as Culross and Falkland, where the majority of old buildings have been restored or sympathetically improved, bring the planners' treatment of Dysart into sharp contrast.

The same survey recorded sixty shops in Dysart High Street, with forty-one food shops including different Co-op departments and the rest made up of shops such as drapers, shoemakers and ironmongers.

Royal Burgh Tavern, c. 1920.

At the end of 1996 there were just three remaining: post office, general store, and licensed grocer.

*Pan Ha',
c. 1890.*

Fortunately for future generations, several of the finest old buildings escaped the onslaught and were not only preserved but given a new lease of life. Several of them were built in the time of James VI and I, when the burgh was enjoying a time of prosperity, and when wealthy merchant shipowners used skilled craftsmen and the best materials to build substantial houses.

The most ambitious piece of renovation was completed in 1969 at Pan Ha', a group of old houses on the shore, thanks to the vision of several people including Hew Lorimer, then the National Trust for Scotland's representative in Fife. The project came under the NTS Little Houses Restoration Scheme, with the National Trust for Scotland collaborating with the Commissioners for Crown Estates and Kirkcaldy Town Council.

By the early 1960s, the houses, which include some splendid examples of sixteenth to eighteenth century domestic architecture, were mostly in a very poor state of repair; and the scheme was a combination of restoring and modernising six of the houses and building five new homes in a harmonising style to replace demolished buildings. The cost of £100,000, which must have been considered high at the time, was a far-seeing investment in the future of the area.

The residents of the houses, whether tenants or owners, were

Renovation work at Pan Ha', c. 1905.

rehoused, and although the initial plan was to provide homes at "economic rents," at the end of the day the houses were all owner-occupied and, with their uniform white harling and red pantiles, are now considered one of the most desirable addresses in Dysart.

(The scheme was not, incidentally, the first time that restoration work had been done on the houses by the shore. At the turn of the century extensive improvements were made, with outside staircases being done away with and many houses getting new roofs. Throughout the years the harling was regularly freshened up with lime-wash in different colours, which must have given a distinctive look to the shore not unlike the present-day waterfront at Tobermory.)

One of the oldest houses in Pan Ha' is The Anchorage, which was built in 1582 presumably for a wealthy shipowner. It has an anchor-and-rope carved stone on one wall and an inscribed date-stone on another; and comparison with an 1840 wood engraving shows how faithfully the exterior has been preserved. The restored houses have as far as possible been named after their original occupants, including the Tide Waiter's House, the Pilot's House and Shore Master's House.

One of the most interesting houses in the group, and the last to be renovated, was the Bay Horse Inn. Dating back to 1585, the house was built for Patrick Sinclair, son of Lord St Clair. The initials PS were found with a coat of arms on the original painted ceiling which came

*The Anchorage,
1840.*

to light under a newer wooden one when the house was being renovated; and the same initials were carved on a pyramid-shaped stone in the garden. The survival of these two original features (now stored in Edinburgh) and other stones was due to the foreman on the job, James Shirra, who recognised their importance and stopped them from being thrown into the demolition skip.

A good-sized house with stables to the side and a garden, the Bay Horse Inn was built hard up against the old manse of St Serf's, which in turn had other houses built behind it in a square courtyard.

Three corners of the house, just under the eaves, are each ornamented by an unusual carved stone head or skewputt, remarkably

Bay House and St Serf's tower.

Two of the skewputts on Bay House

well preserved. The carvings show the heads of two men and a woman, each with ruffs round their necks, staring impassively across the waters of the Forth. Although the popular story goes that they are Mary, Queen of Scots, Darnley and Henry VIII, historical research points to them being James VI and his consort, Anne of Denmark, with their son Charles (later Charles I).

The grandparents of pre-Raphaelite author and art critic John Ruskin lived in the house for some years at the beginning of the nineteenth century, and may have actually owned it for some time.

Despite its name, it was an inn for only a comparatively short time, from probably about the middle of the nineteenth century to around the turn of this century. Its last licensee was Alexander Keddie, who brought his bride Isabella to the house in 1894. One of their daughters, Mrs Elizabeth Westwater, was born in the house in 1908 and stayed there until she was sixty – the last of the original residents to leave when the row of houses was renovated.

"My father had a plaque up at the side of the house saying 'Alex Keddie, Porter and Ales'," she recalled. "The entrance was through the gateway with the carved lintel, and you went downstairs to the bar, which we called the shop. Next to it was the captains' room, where the ships' captains had their drink, and you can still see the wee window at the front of the building at ground level.

"There were four rooms upstairs with each door leading directly into the next room, although we later had them closed up to give a bit more privacy.

"When I was wee, we used to play in the old building which I believe was the old manse, and we had our boiler and wash-house in the lower part of the building. Eventually they pulled it down in case it fell on my mother when she was doing the washing. There must

Completion of the renovation of Pan Ha' in 1969 with the Queen Mother being presented with a print of Dysart from Councillor Janet Meikle watched by Provost Nicholson of Kirkcaldy.

have been other houses there too, because you could see where the fireplaces had been. There was an old mine shaft in the garden and we used to play in that.

"My five sisters, one brother and I were all born in the house, and I was married in it too; the minister came to the house and my father came through the lobby with me on his arm. The grandchildren were all born there too.

"There was something awfully good about the Bay Horse Inn, we had happy times there. I liked it when we stayed there; Michael Nairn was our first landlord and then it belonged to the town. Someone said we lived in a wee world of our own down there at the shore, and so we did, we were all like one family in some ways."

The completion of the renovation scheme in February 1969 was marked by a visit by Queen Elizabeth, the Queen Mother, who as Patron of the National Trust for Scotland unveiled a commemorative plaque and visited several of the houses.

Another fine sixteenth century house, The Towers in Quality Street, was renovated by Kirkcaldy Town Council in 1965 to form three local authority flats. The staircase tower with its carved wall plaque (CL – KL, 1589) was added to on two separate occasions, probably in the eighteenth and nineteenth centuries, to form the main house and an extension. In its last phase until its restoration, it was home to four successive Dysart doctors. It stands beside another listed building, a smaller house which has a marriage lintel with the initials WB – GB, and the date 1610.

Tucked into a corner of nearby Fitzroy Square is St David's , a category A listed, three-storey L-shaped building which dates back to around 1580 and which has been privately restored. Some fine original interior features still remain, including heavy wooden beams on two ground floor ceilings, a huge stone-built hearth and inglenook, and two fireplaces and a window-seat (possibly to store firewood) in the bedrooms. At one time there was a maids' stair leading from the ground floor to the top of the house; this has now been blocked off but the top step of the stone staircase can still be seen, neatly boxed into the floor.

The Towers, 1886.

Fascinating reminders of the past can also still be seen in little niches set in the thickness of the stone walls, the dovecote within the top floor of the house and now used as an attic, and hints of hidden doorways and cupboards behind the existing plasterwork. Recent repairs showed that the old plaster in one bedroom was bound with horsehair and straw, and work on the roof revealed that the timbers are securely held together with wooden pegs rather than nails. A small outbuilding or barn, also a listed building, stands at the gates in Rectory Lane.

The jewel in the crown of Dysart's historic buildings is the Tolbooth at the Cross. Built in 1576, it incorporated the public weights-and-measures office as well as the guard-house and the prison, and the heavy iron barred doors of the cells are still to be seen. In 1617 the Town Hall was built adjacent to it, replacing St Serf's tower as the place where the Provost and Town Council met once a week. Part of the premises were also rented out as a coffee room in the early 1800s at 30/- a year on a ten-year lease, with facilities for reading newspapers and a subscription library. Carved date stones and an early form of the Burgh Arms can be seen on two sides of the building.

St David's, 1886

In 1656, troops from Cromwell's army were billeted in the Tolbooth and one of them, slightly the worse for drink, dropped a lighted torch into a barrel of gunpowder which had been confiscated

Tolbooth, 1960.

The Jubilee lamp with protective bollards.

from a local merchant. The explosion blew the roof off and severely damaged the building, which stood as a semi-ruin for several years until enough money was raised to repair it.

There has been a clock in the Tolbooth since 1592, and the present mechanism and clock faces date from 1876. The old bell from St Serf's, which had become cracked and faint, was taken down in 1808 and sent to London with the original bell from the Tolbooth; the metals from both were melted down and moulded into the large bell which called the bairns home to bed and which, although now silent, is still housed in the top of the four-storey building.

There was a well at the foot of the Tolbooth stairs which for many years was the chief water supply for the houses and harbour; the brass fittings and commemorative plaque marking the well disappeared in the 1960s.

In 1887, the year of Queen Victoria's Golden Jubilee, the Town Hall was replaced and the buildings below and adjacent in Victoria Street (which had its name gentrified at the same time from Flesh Wynd where the abattoir stood) were used as the police station, cells and police houses. To commemorate the Jubilee an ornamental lamp standard was put up just outside the Tolbooth in the middle of the Cross. After it had its third close encounter with heavy traffic in the 1970s it was temporarily removed, but robust local protests ensured its reinstatement and so far it has survived the years.

Another (and possibly the oldest remaining) sixteenth century house stands in Fitzroy Place (formerly The Coalgate), the birthplace in 1815 of John McDouall Stuart who was the first explorer to cross Australia from South to North.

The son of a Customs Officer, Stuart trained as a civil engineer and worked in Glasgow for some time. He fell in love and became engaged to a cousin of his best friend, William Russell; but he arrived at her home one evening just as she was giving Russell a cousinly farewell kiss before he emigrated. Jumping to a hasty conclusion worthy of a romantic novel, Stuart turned on his heel and walked out of his fiancée's life for good, boarding a ship for Australia.

Apparently the young lady later handed Russell her engagement ring with the request that, if he ever met Stuart again, he was to return the ring and explain the misunderstanding. Oddly enough, the two men did meet up again by chance in Adelaide, and the ring was delivered with the message; but there was no reconciliation and Stuart remained a bachelor.

His epic adventures, with dangers from intense heat, attacks by Aborigines, and unknown hazards, are too lengthy to be chronicled here; after five unsuccessful attempts, he eventually led his expedition through the centre of Australia from Adelaide to Dar-

John McDouall Stuart, 1863.

win in 1862, the first time it had been achieved from that direction. His name is commemorated today in the 950-mile Stuart Highway which runs from Alice Springs to Darwin, and in Mount Stuart which stands in the centre of Australia.

His last journey was too much for his health, and he had to be carried for much of the time on the way back. He died in London four years later when he was fifty-one, and was buried in Kensal Green cemetery in London.

Other landmarks however have not survived the years. The Castle O' Guns, a tall 1584 building which probably served as another level of fortification for the Hermitage, was demolished in 1955 to make way for blocks of flats in Howard Place. The original owners are thought to have been John Wardlaw and his wife Janet Keith whose family may have owned the island of Inchkeith. The house was built the year after the Plague came to Dysart, and the couple marked their gratitude at surviving by inscribing "Gif Thankis Unto The Lord, 1585" on the stone lintel with their initials. The elaborately carved stone, which also includes symbols representing the blacksmith's guild, was saved from the demolition and incorporated into the wall of the new flats.

The Castle O' Guns stone, Howard Place.

One of the most recent major demolitions was the Normand Memorial Hall which was built in 1885. It was a gift to the people of Dysart from Sarah Jane Normand, the widow of linen manufacturer James Normand (the son of the first Provost of Dysart).

The cost of the hall and its furnishings was around £5,000, with an additional donation of £1,000 for maintenance. The site on which it was built was known for many years as The Shambles or the Rough Corner, the scene of persistent calls to the local constabulary to deal with nineteenth century drunk-and-disorderly scenes. The building itself was designed in a dignified Renaissance style, with seating accommodation for 363 in the main area and a further 171 in the galleries.

Mrs Normand's original intention was to provide a public hall "for such purposes as will tend to the moral, social and intellectual elevation of the community." She felt very strongly that it was not to be used for purposes which were "not of a distinctly good and wholesome nature." The Town Council held a special meeting to discuss the terms of the deed of gift, particularly a clause which said the hall should never be used "as a dancing saloon or for professional theatrical performances."

The Council debated long and hard about that, with one councillor carefully pointing out that "it does not state that there shall be no dancing," and the Provost saying that it would be a pity to rule out theatrical performances altogether. A compromise was reached; no dancing saloon, but occasional plays by "visiting theatricals."

The foundation stone for the building was laid on 1st March, 1884, with Masonic honours by Captain James Oswald of Dunnikier (Provincial Grand Master) and the Earl of Rosslyn (Past Grand Master). It was by all accounts a very grand occasion, with a procession consisting of the Provost and members of the Town Council, members of Fife Masonic lodges and other societies, and Normand's factory workers, marching from the Cross round the town to the new hall. It was led by the St Clair Band from Dysart, the Pathhead Band, and Kirkcaldy's Trades Band, and passed under banners and flags flying from houses, and evergreen arches at the entrance to the hall. The heavy snowfall in the morning was cleared by a "street sweeping machine" from Kirkcaldy, and as it was a public holiday, the residents turned out in force.

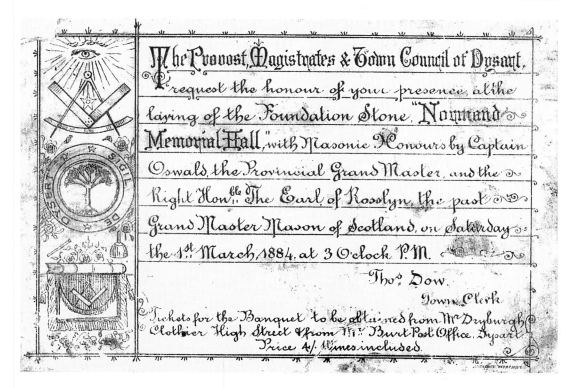

The Provost, Magistrates & Town Council of Dysart, request the honour of your presence at the laying of the Foundation Stone "Normand Memorial Hall", with Masonic Honours by Captain Oswald, the Provincial Grand Master, and the Right Honble The Earl of Rosslyn, the past Grand Master Mason of Scotland, on Saturday the 1st March, 1884, at 3 O'clock P.M.

Thos Dow.
Town Clerk.

Tickets for the Banquet to be obtained from Mr Dryburgh, Clothier, High Street & from Mr Burt Post Office, Dysart. Price 4/- Wines included.

A sealed metal box containing coins of the realm, copies of the *Fife Free Press*, *Kirkcaldy Times* and *The Scotsman*, and an illuminated manuscript written by Thomas Dow, Town Clerk, with the Dysart seal in wax, was buried beneath the foundation stone. After the ceremony a banquet (which, before the days of equal opportunities, was a strictly men-only event) took place in the Fitzroy Hall (now the Masonic Hall) in West Quality Street, with enough speeches and toasts to satisfy the most demanding of Victorian audiences, with songs thrown in for good measure.

Invitation card to Alex Keddie, proprietor of the Bay Horse Inn, to the laying of the foundation stone ceremony.

The building was completed in just over a year, and on 8th May, 1885, the Normand Memorial Hall was officially opened. There was another banquet in the afternoon, with 400 invited guests sitting down to cakes and wine; again it was for men only, although the ladies were permitted to sit in the galleries and look on. The day ended with a concert in the evening by Dysart Musical Association.

The hall was soon in great demand for lectures (illustrated by magic lantern slides), variety concerts and musical events, soirées, flower shows, and social occasions. Although the dancing saloon ban was upheld, a much more genteel Volunteer Ball was held by the Fife Artillery Volunteers, with the platform decorated with plants from the conservatories in Dysart House and, according to the local paper, "a novel arrangement of gas jets representing a crown and, at the other end of the gallery, the Prince of Wales' feathers." One corner of the

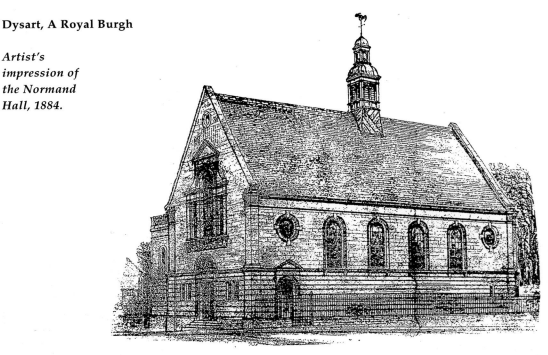

hall was "artistically portioned off as the refreshment rooms, screened off with a netting of flowers and entrance being gained by two beautiful bowers. On the whole, the hall was decorated beyond anything yet seen in the ancient burgh."

For the coming-of-age party in 1890 for Lord Loughborough (later the 5th Earl of Rosslyn), the hall and gallery were again decorated with banks of plants, and a band from Edinburgh played all night. It was also the venue for a "treat for the poor and infirm people of Dysart" to mark Queen Victoria's Golden Jubilee in 1887. Around 200 people were entertained to "a substantial tea" at Mrs Normand's expense, and each given a half-pound packet of tea going out the door. Ten years later, at the Queen's Diamond Jubilee, the hall was used to distribute free parcels of beef, potatoes, sugar and tea.

Within a few years of its opening, there was some disappointment being expressed that the Normand Hall was not being used as extensively as it had been hoped. Various factors were considered; local groups thought that the charges of 10/-, plus 5/- for the hall keeper (with a higher rate for dinners and late night events) were too high. It was also felt that the hall was too big for "ordinary purposes," and that existing church halls were being used for smaller gatherings.

From about 1916 it was used as a cinema and this continued with declining attendances until 1957. By then it was being given only occasional use, mainly as a youth club, until it was allowed to fall into disrepair. It stood derelict for many years, with various plans such as being turned into sheltered housing, taken over by the National Trust for Scotland, or bought by private developers, coming to nothing. Eventually, although a category B listed building, the hall was demolished for safety reasons in 1995.

The site, on the corner of High Street and Rectory Lane, was redeveloped as the Normand Memorial Garden and officially opened in June 1996 by Richard Normand, MC WS, the great-grandson of James Normand, Provost of Dysart. Children from Dysart Primary School made an audio tape and a booklet about their life and times and these, together with other items supplied by The Dysart Trust, were placed in a modern-day time capsule which was buried in the garden. The opening ceremony, which was organised by the Trust included music by the Dysart Colliery Silver Band with long-serving member Harry Briggs, songs by school pupils, and the planting of a cherry tree by Mr Normand.

Directly opposite the Normand Memorial Garden is an interesting row of cottages, built around 1900 as offices for the Earl of Rosslyn's collieries with accommodation for the colliery manager. They were sold when the Fife Coal Company took over the pits, and are now in private ownership.

There is now little trace of the great days of steam when the railway came to Dysart in 1846. The Town Council opposed the idea when it was first introduced a year previously; their main objection was that a great deal of money had been spent making the wet dock at the harbour, and that the railway would take away its trade. They also complained that there was no provision for a branch line to the harbour as had been planned for both Kirkcaldy and Kinghorn.

After some wrangling, the Edinburgh and Northern Railway Company bought the Town's Garden land for £1,800 to build tracks and a station. The name Edinburgh and Northern did not survive for long; in 1849 it changed its name to Edinburgh, Perth and Dundee, and in 1862 it was swallowed up by the North British Railway company. The provision of the railway opened up travel for local people, and the station saw the start of many excursions and holidays. There was also a link with the Frances Pit, with a siding being built in 1879 from the station to the pit, a distance of 1860 yards.

In 1880 the Council pressed for improvements to be made to the station with a waiting room built on the north side of the platform. Three years later, when the railway company had still not provided this, the Council discussed the matter. "It is a very fair and reasonable request," said Provost Watt. "Some of the passengers got very heavy colds by standing at the station waiting for the trains, which were very often late."

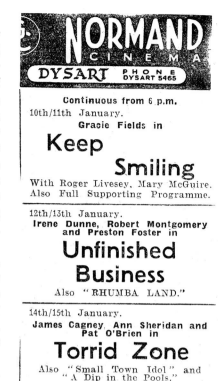

Advertisement for Normand Cinema, 8th January 1949.

Dysart Station.
There was also understandable local resentment about the fact that cheap Saturday fares to Edinburgh were provided from neighbouring Sinclairtown and Kirkcaldy stations, but not Dysart. It took repeated requests over more than ten years before the concession was finally granted.

After the initial tussles and arguments to bring the railway to the burgh in the first place, the station was axed by British Railways just over 120 years later as part of the Beeching plan.

Another long-gone service is the tramcar, when the rails were extended from Kirkcaldy to Dysart in 1911 to the terminus in Townhead, opposite McLeod the saddler's on the same side as the Barony Church. The route ran along Dysart Road down the Path or via St Clair Street to Dunnikier Road, Victoria Road and Factory Road. The trams had a short life; and by 1931 buses had taken over in popularity.

The area overlooking the shore behind and beside Pan Ha' has seen a drastic change over the years. Single storey sheltered houses have replaced the row of tenements at Edington Place, whose gardens are thought to have marked the line of the old town wall. Gone too are the Dovecote Crescent houses on Piper's Braes, the subject of compulsory purchase orders in 1966 when the Coal Board needed more

The first tram into Dysart, 11th January 1911

c. 1920.

Dovecot Houses, Dysart.

M. 114.

Dubbie Braes café, c. 1905.

Man I' the Rock, 1908.

land to dump the redd from the Frances. Also gone from the shore-line are the not so picturesque gasworks, although fierce storms in December 1995 uncovered (for the first time for many years) part of the wall which protected the gasworks from the sea. There is now little trace of the golden sands which once provided residents and visitors with prime spots for family beach games and picnics. The café on the Dubbie Braes, which was built around 1900 on the site of two cannons from the Crimean War, is also gone; rented from the local authority, its last tenant was George Cascarino (who also owned two chip shops and an ice cream café in the High Street) until it burned down in 1931.

Another landmark which has disappeared from the shore is the now legendary 'Man I' the Rock,' a sculpture of a man chained to a rock and carved out of the natural soft sandstone. It was made in 1851 by John Paterson, a local handloom weaver, and was inspired by Byron's poem *The Prisoner of Chillon*. Over the years the sandstone was affected by erosion and the carving finally fell into the sea in 1970.

The present day Old Rectory Inn, which was built as a manse probably in the early 1800s, stands on part of a piece of ground which was given to the clergy of St Serf's before the Reformation. The piece of land was itself known as The Rectory, and stretched from West Quality Street down to the old colliery offices in the High Street. In the 1890s the rector, who was chaplain to the Earls of Rosslyn, was moved to the Rosslyn Chapel when the estate passed out of the St Clair family's hands.

Opposite the Old Rectory in West Quality Street, two houses which like the Normand Hall were allowed to deteriorate past the point of no return, were demolished in 1996. The cottage at No 1 was built in the mid-1600s and was sometimes known as the Gardener's House, as there was an extensive market garden behind it (between the present Community Hall and the children's playpark.) The three-storeyed house next to it was built around 1723 for the St Clair family after the Hermitage burned down, to give them accommodation until Dysart House was built. It was then occupied by the factor of the Rosslyn estate until the 1930s.

The sheer scale and short-sightedness of the post-war redevelopment has in retrospect saddened many residents as well as visitors. While nothing can bring back the lost architectural and historic heritage, it can only be hoped that lessons have been learned and that the past excesses of demolition will never be repeated.

Dysart's past is an intricate, complex one, and Dysart today is very different from what it was a hundred or even fifty years ago. Time alone will tell whether future historians will judge it to be an improvement.

It's encouraging to see that local people in recent years have not only felt a deep appreciation of their heritage but have also voiced their concerns where this has been threatened; and that their views are now being listened to and, in many cases, acted upon by local government and national historic bodies.

Going hand in hand with this is a realisation that the key to the future lies in today's youngsters, who by keeping a sense of community pride can ensure that Dysart remains a very special place in the minds and hearts of generations to come.

Selective Bibliography

(Many of these books are now out of print, but most can be obtained in local libraries.)

Dear Duchess, by Denis Stuart (pub Victor Gollancz)
Dysart (J. Priestley)
Dyart Past and Present, by Andrew S. Cunningham
Dysart Primary School: Log Book Extracts
Dysart Trail, The, by Jim Swan (pub The Dysart Trust)
Dysart: Village History and Walkabout (pub Wemyss Environmental Education Centre)
Fife Coal Company Ltd, The, by Augustus Muir
Heroic Journey of John McDouall Stuart, The, by Ian Mudie (pub Angus and Robertson)
John McDouall Stuart, by Mona Stuart Webster (pub Melbourne University Press)
Mining in the Kingdom of Fife, by Andrew S. Cunningham
My Gamble with Life, by the Earl of Rosslyn (pub Cassells)
Recollections of Dysart, by Alexander Logan
Twice Captured, by the Earl of Rosslyn